W9-CHA-811

Praise for *Mobilized Marketing*

"I've been lucky enough to have been doing mobile for about as long as it's been a viable marketing channel and touch point. I was thrilled when I found out Jeff was writing this book since I knew full well the story hadn't yet been told. And I also believed there was no one better suited and positioned to tell it than Jeff, looking back and forward from his prime seat at the head of the table at Hipcricket.

"Jeff's unique role in our industry's origin stories affords him superb and actionable insights about where we're heading. Jeff gets that mobile is not one thing—it isn't just 'little digital.' It isn't just apps or messaging. And it certainly isn't just about media. He gets the big picture—that what's really going on is a new era of brand marketing and human behaviors that is best summed up by what some of us call 'mobilityness.' Jeff gets that mobilityness matters, and this book is about the how and the why. It is a tale both instructive and inspirational as it uncovers the key lessons learned over the past 10 years of early mobile and point us toward the opportunities which lie ahead for the future of all marketing, with mobile as its beating heart."

—Thom Kennon,
senior vice president, director of strategy, Y&R

"Jeff is a superb storyteller and in this book he takes you through the story of mobile and its place within the marketing mix. At every step along the way, he shares key lessons and insights that will help you ask the right questions and know how to get the right answer. Jeff will prepare you to embrace mobile in a way that will help you deliver value to your customers, your employer, and your career."

—Michael Becker,
managing director for North America,
Mobile Marketing Association
(from the foreword of *Mobilized Marketing*)

"Mobile marketing is about giving your customer the right message via the right channel at the right time. When it works well, nothing is more intimate and effective. Jeff knows what works. And the stories from mobile marketing leaders he features in this book add detail and dimension to Jeff's compelling strategic insights. It's a fast, informative, entertaining read, and it will set you up with a clear point of view on the latest mobile thinking.

"If you want your audience to pick up their phones and engage with your brand, you need to pick up this book!"

—**Miles Orkin,**
former national director, Web and mobile,
American Cancer Society

"Jeff puts the power and potential of mobile marketing into a whole new light. His knowledge and expertise jumps off every page. *Mobilized Marketing* provides a roadmap of lessons, ideas, and applications. Perhaps even more important is Jeff's passion for the promise of where the mobile platform is leading marketing. It's infectious."

—**Hank Wasiak,**
owner, The Concept Farm, and former vice chairman,
McCann Erickson WorldGroup

"When looking for insight and direction, ask the expert. Jeff Hasen is the top thought leader in mobile marketing. He offers strategic direction, informative case studies, and practical advice for mobile marketing. Mobile marketing is the next frontier in how to reach and serve the needs of customers."

—**Mary Furlong,** pre-eminent marketer to Boomers

"A trusted and valuable partner of mine and the Hipcricket team, Jeff has long been an advocate of pragmatic mobile programs that drive business results. From his 'insider' vantage point, Jeff has the case studies and insights that will make you more successful. Plus, his background as a journalist ensures that we get the best from more than two dozen marketers Jeff interviewed who have taken the mobile road and now provide lessons that we can use."

—**Ivan Braiker,**
founder and president, Hipcricket

Mobilized Marketing

How to Drive Sales, Engagement, and Loyalty Through Mobile Devices

Jeff Hasen

WILEY

John Wiley & Sons, Inc.

Copyright © 2012 by Jeff Hasen. All rights reserved.

Published by John Wiley & Sons, Inc., Hoboken, New Jersey.

Published simultaneously in Canada.

For general information on our other products and services or for technical support, please contact our Customer Care Department within the United States at (800) 762-2974, outside the United States at (317) 572-3993 or fax (317) 572-4002.

Wiley publishes in a variety of print and electronic formats and by print-on-demand. Some material included with standard print versions of this book may not be included in e-books or in print-on-demand. If this book refers to media such as a CD or DVD that is not included in the version you purchased, you may download this material at http://booksupport.wiley.com. For more information about Wiley products, visit www.wiley.com.

Library of Congress Cataloging-in-Publication Data:

Hasen, Jeff, 1958-
   Mobilized marketing : how to drive sales, engagement, and loyalty through mobile devices/ Jeff Hasen.
      p.   cm.
   ISBN 978-1-118-24326-8 (cloth); ISBN 978-1-118-28705-7 (ebk);
   ISBN 978-1-118-28314-1 (ebk); ISBN 978-1-118-28423-0 (ebk)
      1. Telemarketing.   2. Mobile commerce.   3. Internet marketing.   4. Cell phone advertising.   I. Title.
   HF5415.1265.H378   2012
   658.8'72—dc23
                                                          2012003558

Printed in the United States of America

10 9 8 7 6 5 4 3 2 1

This book is dedicated to the most supportive mother one could hope to have; to the memory of my father, who is with me every minute of every day; and to my wife, Kathryn, who personifies partner and shares in this achievement.

Contents

Acknowledgments

Fortunately Hipcricket has many "raving fans"—clients who view us as partners rather than vendors. That surely is a testament to my talented colleagues. I'm a raving fan of the clients featured in this book as well as others who have taught me about real business challenges and mobile's ability—or in some cases inability—to make a difference.

My fellow senior executives at Hipcricket have supported my work at the company and the writing of this manuscript. In particular, Paul Arena, Ivan Braiker, Eric Harber, Tom Virgin, and Doug Stovall have created and cultivated the collaborative culture that makes an endeavor like this possible.

Philippe Poutennet, our marketing director, provided important global and U.S. perspectives for this work as well as all the support one could want.

The team at fama PR deserves my deep gratitude. Calling an agency an extension of your team sounds trite, but in this case, it's 100 percent accurate. Special thanks to Ed Harrison, who should be listed on Wikipedia as the ideal PR counsel and friend, as well as Nicole Cromwell and Keri Bertolino, who, like Ed, view our success as their own.

Shannon Vargo from John Wiley & Sons, Inc., has believed in this project from the beginning and has provided invaluable insights and support. Elana Schulman has been there at every step, and I thank her for her time and patience. I also salute the efforts of my production editor, Lauren Freestone.

I have wonderful support from friends, colleagues, and others all across the globe. Special thanks go to Mario Schulzke, Mary Furlong, Hank Wasiak, Joy Liuzzo, Gay Gabrilska, Valerie Clay, Ken Manche, Zach Braiker, Mickey Alam Khan, Jeannine Woodyear, Michael Becker, Vivian Riley, Jean Walker, and Bob Walker.

My family is at the heart of everything I do and everything that I'm about. My brothers, Darryl and Rick, are special beyond words. Mom shows strength thought to be possessed only by superheroes. I have special appreciation for my wife, Kathryn, who believes in me and in us, and fuels our growth.

Foreword

This book could not have arrived at a better time. Today, life itself is mobile. Just look around you.

There are more than 10 billion mobile, connected devices in use around the world, and we're just getting started. Nearly everyone—more than likely you and definitely me included (I have four devices with me nearly all the time)—uses one or more mobile devices daily. These include feature phones and smartphones, tablets, gaming devices, e-readers, and more. We're using these devices to meet the demands of our daily lives.

What are we all doing? We're living. We're texting and talking with our friends and colleagues, playing a game, watching a movie (I can't live without my streaming Netflix account), checking in, searching for information—store hours, locations, and the latest deal—and buying goods and services at unprecedented rates. Our mobile devices have become our computer, portal to the Internet, watch, radio, television, newspaper, book, magazine, camera, shopping list, and so much, much more.

Life has become mobile. Consequently, so must marketing. Mobile marketing is an indispensable part of the marketing mix, and it is imperative that every brand and retail marketer learn how to integrate mobile practices into their overall marketing efforts.

Don't believe me? Let Jeff show you. You're in for a treat. This is a book for everyone, no matter how big or small their business, no matter which industry they work in or their place within their organization, and—most important—no matter how much experience they already have with mobile. There is something for everyone within its covers.

Jeff is a superb storyteller, and in this book, he takes you through the story of mobile and its place within the marketing mix. At every step along the way, he shares key lessons and insights that will help you ask the right questions and know how to get the right answer. Jeff will prepare you to embrace mobile in a way that will help you deliver value to your customers, your employer, and your career.

Jeff shares with the reader how, from an inspired spark of innovation, the wildfire that is mobile took off, transforming the fabric of society and forever changing how we live our lives. In these pages Jeff has captured the essence of mobile's impact on marketing and mobile's place within the marketing mix.

Jeff brings mobile marketing to life by providing real-world context as he explains how and why it works; for example, how a marketer can reshape a simple traditional media branding campaign into a loyalty-generating, imitative, strategic program that materially benefits the bottom line.

That's hugely useful. I know from talking to thousands of marketers that jumping into mobile marketing can be daunting. Marketers don't want to get into the game late, but this may also be tempered by a reluctance that without clear data on return on investment (ROI), investing in mobile may be premature. Marketers should recognize that in mobile's incredible growth (an estimated annual growth rate of 50 percent for 2012) is clear evidence of mobile's success and staying power. Now is the time for marketers to plan for updating spend and integrating mobile into the marketing mix.

In the pages that follow, Jeff proves that case and tells you how to make mobile work for you. He shares the insights of leading industry executives and his own personal experiences, and details numerous case studies, which span a wide range of industries and objectives. Jeff shares with the reader detailed explanations of what works and what doesn't, and provides insight as to how every marketer can start embracing some or all aspects of mobile marketing, today, without fear.

—**Michael Becker**
Managing Director, North America
Mobile Marketing Association

Preface

In 1965 Maxwell Smart made what I believe to be the first wireless call. Although others in that era may have thought shine when considering their shoes, Smart viewed his footwear as a device best suited to delivering an apology.

"Sorry about that, Chief," the bumbling spy often cried out on shoe-phone calls to his disappointed boss on *Get Smart*, an American television comedy created by Mel Brooks and Buck Henry.

The show had an entertaining five-year run and won seven Emmy Awards, yet Smart's phone feat is often overlooked when the early history of the mobile device is discussed.

The Motorola DynaTAC is frequently called the first commercially available wireless phone—apparently Maxwell Smart received his shoe phone not through a retail store but via his connections as a secret agent.

Known widely as the brick and made famous by Michael Douglas's Oscar-winning character Gordon Gekko in the film *Wall Street*, the DynaTAC weighed 2½ pounds, contained 30 circuit boards, and was 9 inches tall. It cost $3,995 at the time, which is equivalent to $8,724 today, according to Motorola.

It took 10 hours to recharge, and one could talk no more than 30 minutes before the power was gone.

One could understand Gordon Gekko's need for power. When it comes to mobile devices, the power desire is hardly unique.

Today, billions around the world turn to their cell phones 24 hours a day—as alarm clocks, for daily computing tasks, as pipelines to their friends and family down the block and around the world, and increasingly as the vehicle to interact with brands, be it as part of a loyalty club or to research products and services and make purchases.

The last of the activities mentioned has the largest ramifications for marketers.

Mobilized Marketing introduces you to people just like you who have—and continue to face—business challenges in this rapidly changing, technologically advancing, "time-crunched" society, as Kris Foley of Clear Channel Cleveland describes it.

Some of the folks you will meet are pioneers who founded or furthered Hipcricket, one of the leading mobile marketing and advertising companies in the world that set out to save or reinvigorate struggling industries and to drive others to new heights.

You will be introduced to brand marketers just like you. Fate seemingly brought some of them to mobile. Foresight, smarts, and, yes, more than a little bit of risk-taking drove others into the dynamic world of mobile. Their results will astound and inspire you.

We'll consider the radio sales manager in Baltimore who sold mobile into an auto dealer's radio schedule and produced 34 car sales in one day after the dealer had not sold one in more than a month; the American Red Cross, which saved lives by using mobile to remind blood donors to give so others could receive; and Ford and its dealers, which drove a 14 percent lead conversion rate by adding mobile to its rich, yet previously mobile-lacking, traditional advertising programs.

This book will allow you to see what these marketers saw and apply those lessons to your own careers. You will be better equipped to identify the opportunities, ask the right questions, sell mobile into your organizations, and most important, move the needle on your business.

Mobilized Marketing is not a tome full of hype. It tells the stories of real marketers who made decisions—right or wrong—that provide valuable lessons for us—lessons like: Proceed, give it all you've got, but be smart.

"You have to be prepared to set yourself up to fail but do it in a measured way," Miles Orkin, formerly of the American Cancer Society, tells us in the pages ahead. "Don't bet that you will be the next Mark Zuckerberg [who founded Facebook]. If you fail, you will be selling coffee. So we didn't bet the whole nest egg."

And neither should you. Hipcricket has never advocated recklessness. But we're in mobile—and you should be, too. It has been—and promises to continue to be—one heckuva ride.

PART I

The Early Years

SELL MORE BEER.

Since 1855 it has been the marketer's reason for being at MillerCoors and its predecessor companies.

The job existed before radio's invention in the late nineteenth century, before television came into our ancestors' homes in the 1920s, and before Internet development began in the mid-twentieth century. There certainly was no digital media vying for consumer attention in the bygone eras.

The common thread between Steve Mura and those in marketing positions at MillerCoors before him is a daily need to have meaningful interactions with customers and prospects.

Mura, now director of digital marketing at MillerCoors, learned those lessons right out of Bradley University in Peoria, Illinois, and used them through marketing and promotions positions at Sara Lee and ConAgra Foods.

"I started doing event marketing when I was young in my 20s, and the thing I liked about it was it really allowed you this great opportunity to almost bring a blue-collar mind-set to a white-collar world," says Mura. "Event marketing is very much getting out there at fairs, festivals, and events and I loved that sort of one-on-one interaction. I loved the fact that at those places, fast talk and marketing speak and MBAs [masters of business administration] and all that stuff didn't matter. It was about your opportunity to connect with the true consumer and that was really plain talk and creating connections. That has stayed with me over my whole career.

"Marketing is just that—connecting with consumers, connecting your brand with consumers—and the more plain talk and the more you can convey sort of a realness and a genuineness with your brand, the better off you are. I love that interaction and challenge of being authentic and real, and having products that deliver on your promise."

1

Radio's Days of Glory

THERE WAS A DAY when radio had an enormous promise all its own.

With 14,000 stations in the United States alone, in the largest cities and most remote outposts, the medium and its people were able to deliver on a local level what marketer extraordinaire Seth Godin calls the building of *tribes*. Godin's notion of tribes is any group of people, large or small, who are connected to one another, a leader, and an idea. Radio was one of those ideas. Listeners would gather around transistor receivers, disc jockeys would form bonds with station followers, and, importantly for advertisers, dedicated and passionate audience members would buy soap, car insurance, and yes, even beer, in response to the commercials, promotions, and reviews from others.

Important news was learned via the radio, such as the assassination of U.S. President John F. Kennedy in 1963. The Beatles started a sensation in the same era through no small role of radio. Generations sat side-by-side transfixed on a box that delivered every pitch of World Series mastery by Bob Gibson and Sandy Koufax.

The community nature of radio is what pushed Ivan Braiker into the business in the 1970s.

"Radio in those days was all about engagement," he recalls. "If you think about the way it was growing up 30 years ago or longer, people grew up loving their radio stations and having a great affection for the on-air personalities and having an attachment to the music they played and to the contests.

"With your circle of friends, one of the things you likely had in common was your radio station. Whether it was the Top 40 station or the hard rock station, you were defined by the friends you hung out with."

Braiker had a decorated, 30-year broadcasting career that began much the way Mura's did—by Braiker turning to the basics.

Hired out of school by the CBS Television affiliate in 1972, Braiker immediately broke the mold in his new sales job.

"Being young and just one on the team, no one told me I was supposed to be playing golf at 2 o'clock in the afternoon," he recalls, jabbing at his sales counterparts who would be more apt to find the sun than the next advertiser. "So I worked. Within 90 days, I was the highest billing account executive."

That work ethic and a sense of adventure led him to leadership and ownership of radio stations and groups, and the cofounding and presidency of Satellite Music Network, the first radio network to distribute live, 24-hour programming via satellite. It was an innovation that earned him *Billboard* magazine's Trendsetter of the Year award.

Then, depending on how you view it, either technology came around to spoil radio's party—think choice that listeners never had—or the arrival of the Internet, mobile phone, and digital lifestyles presented radio with opportunities Braiker argues it has not yet, if at all, fully seized.

Despite being in traditional media throughout his career, Braiker was an early adopter of mobile devices and the coming tsunami of change happening via advancements in personal technology.

"I was there with each generation of cell phone," Braiker says. "I was one of the first on my block to own the brick [Motorola's DynaTAC that was introduced in 1983 and considered by many to be the initial wireless phone] and one of the first on the block to own the StarTAC [sold by Motorola to consumers in 1996], which was a mere $1,800 cheaper than the brick.

"Think about what these phones did—it's like comparing a calculator with a computer, yet they cost so much more."

2

Hipcricket's Beginnings in a Starbucks

WELL-CONNECTED IN HIS HOMETOWN to Seattle's venture community and up for a new challenge, Braiker remembers a friend asking him in 2003 if he would meet with an Australian to learn more about a mobile marketing service for radio taking hold Down Under. There, radio stations and listeners were using the text messaging feature of wireless phones to maintain and strengthen their tribes.

It turned out that it was a match made for Braiker.

Braiker's planned 30-minute meeting at Starbucks with Graham Knowles, himself a longtime radio veteran, lasted 8 hours.

"I was so intrigued by what they were doing in Australia," he says. "I couldn't fathom that this wasn't going to be the savior for radio [in the United States]."

Why he believed that radio needed a savior is a complicated question, but a quick look at what was going on in 2004 reveals a world full of changes:

- A social networking site called Facebook launches.
- The last Oldsmobile rolls off the assembly line.
- Google's initial public offering takes place.

If you still need more convincing that the planets were realigning, consider the fact that the Boston Red Sox won the World Series for the first time since 1918, breaking the so-called Curse of the Bambino that began when Babe Ruth was sold to the archrival New York Yankees.

3

Mobile at the Start of the Millennium

AT THE TURN OF the twenty-first century, mobile had gained traction in some areas of the world and wasn't even on call to be a communications device or eventually a mini-computer and entertainment option in others. Those marketers who noticed the increase in wireless usage mostly treaded lightly when it came to the notion of trying to marry a brand's business goals with mobile, which unbeknownst to many of them would soon become a consumer's most personal and often treasured device.

According to CTIA–The Wireless Association, there were nearly 110 million mobile subscribers in the United States alone by the end of 2000. Although that number was impressive for the day, it was dwarfed by wireless adoption in other parts of the world, especially Japan and Korea and in parts of Europe where it came to be that figuratively a ringtone—the sound made when a cell phone receives a call—was heard around the world.

"When did mobile become meaningful in Europe and what was behind it?" says Peggy Anne Salz, an American living in Germany who has gone on to become one of the world's top wireless analysts and commentators. "One word, well two—Crazy Frog. The early driver of mobile was not so much communications as it was entertainment. Europe had what it took to help companies across the mobile entertainment ecosystem develop and flourish. It ranged from interoperability through SMS [text messaging available across mobile operators] and MMS [multimedia messaging] long before the United States, to operator billing and other payment mechanisms, which was the foundation for a sustainable business model, although operators took the lion's share of the revenues, and a huge appetite for mobile downloadable content.

"This annoying ringtone still echoes in the corners of my brain. It broke records across Europe (the product of Germany's Jamba, which was later bought by Fox Mobile). Unfortunately, it also broke a fantastically lucrative business model: the mobile content subscription. Users were confused about the conditions of the deal. What were they getting into? How much did it cost really for the ringtone and data charge? How could they cancel the subscription?"

In the United States in the late 1990s, the Weather Channel sprung into mobile through pagers, a Palm Pilot application, and even one of the earliest mobile Web products. Be it the weather in a hometown or at a business trip destination, a monetizable number of mobile subscribers were interested in having the local conditions and forecast in their pockets.

"There has been one major change with how people use phones but for the most part there has been a lot of consistency with data usage—the top use category is e-mail, then weather, then news, then sports, then comes finance and entertainment," says Louis Gump, a pioneer from his days as vice president of mobile at the Weather Channel and leadership positions on the board of directors of the Mobile Marketing Association. "It has been very consistent over time with just the magnitude changing. One asterisk on that is social because the Facebooks of the world weren't a big deal five to seven years ago on mobile devices and now they're huge."

"What you were selling back then were a couple of products—we tried to sell the mobile Web," remembers Doug Stovall, who began in mobile in the late 1990s with a systems integrator called Xpedior before eventually joining Hipcricket as senior vice president of sales and client services in 2009. "Candidly we had mobile Web products that did the same thing that the mobile Web products do today. The network speeds were so bad and the phones were so bad, it was just a horrible user experience. But we were successful in selling some here and there.

"The other thing we would sell were a lot of synchronization products—think syncing your Palm Pilot to the desktop. You would build an app [application or program] that would do something there. Most of these were not consumer or marketer sells. They were sells to the enterprise [business customers]. We would sell things like synchronization of the enterprise CRM [customer relationship management] systems so the employees could use it."

Eric Harber, who would later go on to become president and chief operating officer of Hipcricket, was similarly making enterprise sales at the time following his MBA studies at Stanford University. Harber's road led him to mobile players Motricity and Qpass, among other businesses, and to the mobile content model that Salz was experiencing in Europe.

"I felt there would be a much broader opportunity if we could tap into larger marketing and advertising spends and a space for large brands to reach their customers and their prospects," he says. "That wasn't going to be via a ringtone download although a lot played that game and did a sponsored ringtone. [It was] get your favorite ringtone from your favorite brand. [But] you can only put so many jingles for Kellogg's cereal on your mobile phone. You could question whether anybody was going to do that anyway.

"So I said, 'What is the next evolution, the step in the market if we're going to go from content, which we saw a huge run-up on content and then it kind of tapered off, what's the next evolution?' I felt the next evolution was a way to engage with customers and prospects with a device that was personalized and always with them."

4

American Idol Engages a Nation

IN THE UNITED STATES, mobile eventually became more of a must-have consumer device primarily for three reasons: the television talent show *American Idol* integrated text into its voting process in 2003 during its second season; text messaging was made available as a cross-carrier product, allowing cell phone users to reach anyone with a mobile device with a messaging capability regardless of the mobile operator that the subscriber chose; and Motorola introduced what became the best-selling RAZR, a clamshell phone that was thin, capable, and an instant fashion statement.

Ten years after the world's first commercial text message was sent by employees of LogicaCMG, just how dramatic was texting's growth because of *American Idol*, which had become one of TV's highest-rated shows?

More than 7.5 million *American Idol*-related text messages were sent by AT&T Wireless customers throughout the 2003 season, including polls, sweepstakes entries, trivia, and votes, according to numbers released by the carrier. More than one-third of all participants had never even sent a text message as an AT&T Wireless customer before *American Idol*. The number of text votes received increased by nearly

5,000 percent from the first voting episode to the last voting episode. More than 2,300 text messages per second were processed at one point during the voting.

American Idol eventually stopped breaking out its vote totals by text versus online. By the end of Season 10 in the spring of 2011, a total of 4.8 billion votes had been cast over the decade of programming. Clearly, messaging via mobile devices had played a major role in the show's success, but the story was much broader than that. In 2009, texting eclipsed voice as the leading daily activity on wireless devices. In 2010, 2.1 trillion text messages were sent and received in the United States, stats from CTIA–The Wireless Association reveal.

Key Takeaways

- It took traditional media to get text messaging to go mainstream.
- *American Idol* wisely used text messaging because the great majority of viewers had the capability on their devices.
- The fact that multiple generations watch *American Idol* together pushed up the average age of texting.
- The least sexy mobile application—short message service (SMS)—was the tool to make *American Idol* cool.

Having read about *American Idol*'s success—or maybe hearing about it via text—the Academy of Television Arts & Sciences hired Hipcricket in 2004 to provide a Mobile Emmy Awards Trivia Challenge and attract the attention of 18- to 34-year-olds. With a first-prize of a trip to the Emmy's the following year, the text-based trivia quizzes ran for 10 days, culminating the night of the Emmy Awards broadcast.

To play, mobile users sent a text message to EMMYS (36697) with the keyword *Play* in the body of the message. The Mobile Emmy Awards Trivia Challenge was promoted in various online/offline media, including *TV Guide, People Magazine, Soap Opera Digest, Soap Opera Weekly,* and the websites for ABC and the Emmy's, among others.

It made sense that mass properties like *American Idol* and the Emmy Awards turned to mobile. Industry records show that the number of U.S. mobile subscribers totaled 34 million in 2005, impressive but still about one-ninth of those who carried wireless devices in 2011.

5

RAZR Sharpens Mobile's Focus

"MOBILE PHONES WERE VERY distinctly phones until the introduction of the Motorola RAZR [in 2004]," says Joy Liuzzo, vice president and director of the research company InsightExpress. "Until that time, phones were bulky and not easy to take with you everywhere without needing a purse or belt holder. The RAZR became the phone you could slip into your back pocket and reach for no matter where you were.

"It also paved the path of a slicker user interface and more focus on the features outside of talking than previous phones. The Motorola RAZR was the gateway drug to the future smartphones, giving a huge number of people a taste of what was possible."

Louis Gump (see Chapter 3), still at the Weather Channel in those days and now vice president of mobile at CNN, agrees.

"Up until 2003 or 2004, most people saw these devices as a way to make phone calls, often sparingly because of the rates," he says. "There were times people used these devices for something other than that. Then text messaging came along and downloads and ringtones and ringback tones and, all of a sudden, these became more personal devices. As that happened, consumers said, 'Hey, maybe I do want to browse. Maybe I do want to get an app.'"

Among those people who tasted what was possible was Ivan Braiker (see Chapter 1) who made a deal with Graham Knowles and business partner Iain Simms to bring a technology platform to America that would enable marketers, radio station programmers, and sales personnel to interact with mobile subscribers primarily via a prompt to text. As important, campaigns could be set up in mere minutes and be measured in Simms's platform in real time—allowing for optimization and salvation for an advertising spend that might be going wrong.

Of course, the group sought a memorable name and decided on Hipcricket after hearing how cell phones were chirping on the hips of mobile owners in Europe.

With no rate card or, more important, no proof that brands, agencies, and broadcast companies would benefit from mobile, Braiker and a very small team working out of his condominium near Lake Washington called on his vast network of relationships.

"At the time, I didn't think it was a risk getting into mobile," he says. "In retrospect, it was an unbelievably huge risk. It took unbelievable tenacity and endurance to run the race that we're still running."

6

Hipcricket's First Customers

BRAIKER RAN FIRST TO Gus Swanson, who was a one-man marketing department at the leading Top 40 station in Seattle, KUBE 93. The idea was to give listeners an ability to communicate with the station via a short code—a five-digit number tied to text messaging that was designated for KUBE and promoted on the station. Campaigns to push additional listening and advertisers' products and services were constructed and had accompanying keywords such as *pizza* for a pizza sponsor.

The most pedestrian campaigns were among the most successful. Swanson's disc jockeys would call upon listeners to text in the word *pizza* for a discount. Those who did received a text message back that they could show to the cashier at the pizza house. It was all permission-based, following the rules of the carriers and Mobile Marketing Association that prohibit spam.

"We've always been out of the box with our marketing and ways to interact with our listeners," Swanson says. "We are always trying to give the audience another way to communicate with the station. The texting scenario we thought was pretty perfect.

"The KUBE 93 listener is an active adult so the ability to do the quick enter to win a contest and some of the polls we would do on

14

the air and even requests when we had that stigma of being 'I tried to call but the line is busy' . . . this kind of overcame that."

Swanson took a swing at mobile without finding bravery pills.

"With any new technology, there's a little bit of a risk but we also recognized the fact that these are young active adults who were texting among themselves already," he tells me. "I came up the marketing ranks, as I know you did, and you recognize the traditional 'one to many' rule. This gave us a one-to-one relationship so we could interact a little more closely with them—we became a friend instead of this box of speakers just talking with them."

There were other takers but Braiker hardly found a line around his condo from businesses prepared to sign up.

"We built a system that had been designed specifically for radio," he says. "Was using it a risk? I'm sure it was perceived that way. To this very day, I still don't understand why. At that particular time, radio was concerned about losing a quarter rather than collecting the $1,000 bills they were walking over.

"I believe that if radio on a uniform basis embraced what mobile marketing was all about and had done it rapidly when we launched, then radio would be controlling and being at the operating point as to what mobile marketing is all about today. They didn't. They were too afraid to spend money. To this day, it's frustrating. Normally we could get the advertisers to get it before we could get the stations to buy in. The advertisers saw what was there."

One of the first to get it was James Darby, who dreamed of a radio job at age 15 and fulfilled it with positions as automations manager, street reporter, and program director, among others, before becoming chief strategy officer at Federated Media.

"When I look at something like Hipcricket or another texting service, I know there's a cost involved," he says. "Essentially in many ways we're starting a new line of business. For a business to make money in its first year I know is fairly unheard of and then you try to break even in year two.

"This is where we get bogged down in our industry sometimes. We look at these expenses and say there's no way we're going to make money in year one. Yeah, you may not, quite honestly, but how are you going to make money in year two and three if you don't even try it in year one? If you budget correctly and make the assumption that maybe you're not going to make money but you're going to offset it somewhere else in the company, that's how you can justify the costs.

"Most importantly, it's not the physical dollars you bring in on the text budget line. It's also about what are we earning by providing a product to cover a customer who expects you to have it. Whether it's an app or text, if we're not in that game and we don't look like we're in technology and part of what people are using and how they're using it, they will go find it somewhere else."

Like MillerCoors' Mura and Clear Channel's Swanson, Darby craved consumer engagement.

"The reason I love the medium is the one-to-one connection that we can have with customers—and an effective relationship," he says. "But I think what we've missed is the social aspect. All of a sudden there's an emergence of a technology that allows us to be social with a lot more people at a given moment. Radio is crazy for thinking that they do not need to be involved in that."

7

Listening to the Consumer

ACROSS THE COUNTRY, AT one of the most influential radio stations in the country, Clear Channel's Director of Marketing Eileen Woodbury knew that her KIIS-FM audience in Los Angeles was texting.

"Around 2005, I was getting hit on by hundreds—I know I'm exaggerating—of mobile companies," she says. "All the talk was how everything is going to be on your phone. At the time, our company had a local deal in place with a text marketing platform provider but we weren't actively engaged with it.

"I recall my marketing manager reached out to me one day and said, 'I don't know exactly how this works, but please meet with them and see if it's useful to us.' I met with the company and I was a little bit unsure of what they were offering and what it could do to drive results for the station. But so many companies were hitting me up, I thought I better take it seriously and figure it out. I ended up setting meetings with 10 or more companies to learn what it was all about and how it could apply to radio. Not many mobile companies were experts specifically in radio at that time. They didn't come with a, 'This is how you can use it in radio, this is how you can increase ratings,' instruction book. It was really an overall brand marketing strategy that they were pitching."

Woodbury was one of the first to see the potential of mobile messaging.

"As the application and strategy became clearer we were really excited to launch a texting initiative," she says. "We saw the Hipcricket platform as far superior to some of the others for our needs. The Hipcricket platform was basically set up and developed to accommodate several types of contesting and to actually drive ratings. Almost right away we felt a tangible and meaningful return on investment. The listener activity was insane.

"Hipcricket really understood what programming success we were looking for, what the sales needs were, and how everything worked together. The platform made sense for us because it could be as niche or as mass as we wanted. With some other platforms we tried, we were limited in the scope of what we could do. But since signing with Hipcricket, we have yet to be told something can't be done. Once meeting with Hipcricket, many things came together. We were able to connect the dots because their marketing and development team came from the radio business, and their platform was developed with that in mind."

Woodbury saw a new way to grow her station's tribe.

"My mind raced realizing how many ways we could actually connect with listeners in a personal way, especially since there is only so much you can say on the air," she says. "All on-air messages are about the big stuff. Mass targeting. With mobile, we could talk about the smaller, niche things we do with a very specific group of listeners who opted in to receive messages from us. We could communicate with them immediately and to get their feedback immediately. This was a tool we could use to drive ratings, and the more we talked about it, the sponsorship and advertising opportunities were so obvious."

The station hired Hipcricket, and immediately brought them in to educate the local sales and programming teams and to engage the DJs to integrate text into their shows. Also, in an effort to create a singular point of entry for the station's already established online listener loyalty club, Woodbury and the Clear Channel Los Angeles online team worked closely with Hipcricket to create a bridge so the two platforms would communicate with each other. Listeners were soon able to sign up for both simultaneously, making it possible for club members to choose how they want to communicate with the station, be it online, via mobile, or both.

It worked like this. If a listener responded to one of the station's text call to actions, by regulation of the carriers and Mobile Marketing Association, the station was permitted to send the mobile subscriber an additional message. To push engagement, the second text would often read, "Would you like to receive similar offers and information? Text the word *JOIN* to 41027 to be part of KIIS mobile club."

"As soon as we figured out what it could do for us, it was on an absolute fast track," Woodbury says. "We've got to be better at this, we have to use it correctly. Then the competitive nature kicked in and we said, 'We've gotta own this.'

"We wanted to try everything. Obviously there are so many ways to use the platform. We wanted to build clubs so we could communicate those niche things. We also wanted to do contesting. With contesting we use text and it's just enormous. Many actually won't pick up the phone and call a radio station today. I don't know if it's the anonymity that goes along with texting or just that it's simple. More people are using text to enter to win something. When they do text and get a bounceback from us, you are able to engage them in a conversation. It's almost like you're closer to them and more personal. Instead of answering, 'Hi, you're caller number two; Hi, you're caller number three' for a contest, we primarily use text. When someone participates, we respond by saying, 'If you want to get more alerts like this from us, hit us up with a reply.' We've seen the numbers in our clubs go up and to this day, we push out messages to these people. We don't have people opt out very often. I think we've established a rapport."

The rapport obviously extends to Hipcricket.

"Hipcricket is an amazing company," she says. "I've always said this to Ivan and everyone there: 'I don't know how you find the people that you find but they're young, they're smart, they're poised and creative.' And I love that they aren't intimidated in a room of older and sometimes cynical people. It's like a 360-degree company. It's kind of unbelievable to me. It's more than a relationship, it is a sincere partnership, one that I love.

"People say, 'Oh, you just say that because they are your friends.' But it's actually the reverse. We've become friends, because they're so great to work with. We've established a relationship as we've developed kick-ass campaigns together. We brainstorm, we strategize, and even work on product development together. I love the process when working with these guys."

8

The Brands Show Some Interest

From the beginning, Ivan Braiker's business model was to extend beyond the broadcasting companies to brands and advertising and promotions agencies.

It was already happening in London where Thom Kennon, then a founding managing director for multichannel agency Rapp Collins, was running opt-in programs for the likes of the world's largest premium drink company in the world.

"It was a chance to work with some of the biggest brands there were as they were trying to experiment with emerging channels," says Kennon, now senior vice president and director of strategy at Y&R, a member of the WPP network of companies. "We did work for Diageo, a pilot to get people coming out of nightclubs in southeast England who were looking for a great curry place, looking for a jazz band, they were looking for an after-hours joint—we put together a mobile platform for us to be able to drive opt-in to a registered database to people who would receive alerts and be able to reach out to them where they were so they could find the things they were looking for on their mobile devices."

Hipcricket's first brand assignment was with Doritos, which aimed to make its product the "alpha snack" for 12- to 24-year-olds. A text call to action was placed on print, TV, radio, outdoor, and online advertising. Consumers were asked what "inNw?" meant (if not now when?). All participants were entered to win prizes and encouraged to go online to opt-in to the Doritos loyalty club.

Doritos received more than 1,000 messages per day and more than 60,000 messages in total. Twenty-eight percent of the participants joined a loyalty club, according to company figures, giving the brand the ability to remarket to those who were willing to receive additional information and offers.

"Who would've thought of using outdoor boards in the middle of New England in the winter, but the program worked," Braiker says.

Key Takeaways

- Being it was such early days, brands like Doritos were testing mobile for proof of concept.
- Even then, mobile subscribers saw value in joining a permission-based mobile loyalty club.
- The outdoor boards were provocative, generating interest and response.

Mura from MillerCoors explains how his company looked at mobile in those years.

"Our job is to get to some level of scale," he says. "Scale was going to happen with us or without us so our job was to make sure we knew what the potential was if it did scale. So we did lean a little forward and kept an eye on that stuff and, more importantly, if a specific technology or specific platform doesn't scale, often the thinking does.

"Part of the key when you're plugged into this space is to understand why are people gravitating, what can I learn. How can I better connect with them and then you almost develop things that are platform- or technology-agnostic."

Among the early winners in mobile were franchisees, other small business, and companies that built opt-in databases to remarket to those who raised their hands and said, "Yes, I am willing to have a conversation with you."

Swanson's KUBE 93 worked with McDonald's to provide a text-based coupon for a free quarter pounder with cheese at any location in six western Washington counties if listeners texted QPC during a 15-minute period. Two thousand responded and Swanson had the proof he needed to sell more.

"We had a vision to associate with our listeners with a lifestyle piece of technology that they're using that they can now use to interact with their favorite radio station," remarks Swanson. "It's the cost of doing business for us now.

"I don't want to sound naïve or arrogant by any means. The fact of the matter is this particular group of radio stations [Swanson has seven in Seattle] has always believed in offense and not necessarily worrying what our competitors are doing or not doing."

9

Mobile as a Natural Progression

Across the country in Cleveland, Kris Foley and her team at Clear Channel station KISS also were having an epiphany about mobile. For the first time, she says, sales, programming, and management were unanimous in their desire to use a technology to get closer to listeners and to get advertisers to spend with the station.

For Foley, it wasn't a matter of having risk-takers singing the same song—it was more of a natural progression for KISS.

"Personality may have had something to do with it but I think it was more we had a number of things that we needed to improve about the operation of the radio station and texting allowed us to accomplish all of them," she says.

"For an example, we went from where the traditional advertiser purchased a 60-second commercial. With that commercial, the hallmark was you had to say the client's website three times and the phone number three times. That's not how people consume media now. It's either, 'Make the message relevant for me right away and I'll tune in to it or I'm going to tune out from it.' We also have a time-crunched society where people want to be informed as quickly and simply as they possibly can."

Further, Foley saw mobile as a tool to drive additional advertising dollars and to help her fulfill a personal mission.

"People thought of us as innovative because of what Hipcricket brought us to use," she says. "We took a model at the beginning to not try to put a high price tag on programs involving texting. We did it more, 'Okay if you spend x amount of dollars with us in an on-air campaign, you'll get this as an added component to your schedule.' It wasn't so scary—that is by far the best way to start with this because when you have success—local revenue determines what the market value is. When you can walk into places and say this is the exact ROI [return on investment] from a texting campaign, that's what we did and how you get someone's attention.

"I just like the idea of helping companies. My dad is an entrepreneur. He started his own company and I could see the struggles that a small business goes through. In radio, you can actually help the small business become a big company and when it works the right way, you can become the least expensive marketing employee that a company can have. It's a passion."

10

Mobile in the Fight Against Cancer

OF COURSE, PASSION POWERS many other entities, including nonprofits like the American Cancer Society (ACS), the largest voluntary health organization in the United States. Since 1914 the society has had a mission to save lives by helping people stay well, get well, find cures, and fight back.

When Miles Orkin decided to join ACS in 2002, he believed mobile would eventually play a large role in the organization's community outreach and ability to engage with his constituencies the way they engage with each other.

"I believe technology is a tool that helps individuals at the right place and the right time communicate easily and effectively," says Orkin, an early digital marketer who was the American Cancer Society's national director of Web and mobile until early 2012. "Technology should help organizations communicate in the voice and through the channels that the consumer wants to hear them in. I learned that [when working] at *Thrasher* [a skateboarding magazine] by opening mail we received and then speaking in their voice. It allowed us to be on the leading edge."

In 2002, ACS, like many nonprofits, had bureaucracy and slow change as barriers to technology adoption.

"There was no mobile role," he says. "Mobile wasn't relevant in 2002, but I came off of spending two years in Spain where mobile was on the radar. ACS had a website that was barely functional. They brought me in to add more digital expertise to the fund-raising effort. Five years ago, we knew we had to get into mobile. I specifically wanted my title to have e-revenue [electronic revenue] and mobile in it. I knew mobile wasn't well understood but it was where we needed to be.

"It was a really slow build. We focused on fund-raising first. At a nonprofit, the best way to get things done quickly is to show something that could bring in funds."

Orkin's first move was measured, aligning his organization with the Mobile Giving Foundation, a nonprofit group that gave mobile subscribers the ability to donate to nonprofits through a text pledge that would appear on their cell phone bill.

"Text to give seemed to be a relevant tool for us," he recalls. "I wouldn't say that it was a smashing success but it put mobile in people's consciousness. Haiti got exposure for text to give [$32 million was raised for the American Red Cross (ARC) in 2010 after a devastating earthquake, with 95 percent of the consumers who texted in to the Haiti campaign being first-time donors to the organization, according to ARC]. We're never going to be that. Cancer isn't an earthquake, a fire, or a flood. But we thought maybe the phone can help us.

"We ran small pilots only within [ACS] divisions that were interested. We kept the overhead as ridiculously low as possible so we didn't have to be a massive success. You have to be prepared to set yourself up to fail but do it in a measured way. Don't bet that you will be the next Mark Zuckerberg [who founded and became chief executive officer of Facebook]. If you fail, you will be selling coffee. So we didn't bet the whole nest egg."

Key Takeaways

- Marketers like Orkin who believed in mobile's promise did not jump in wildly—they tested and learned.
- The American Cancer Society had specific initial business goals in mind—increase donations was top of the list.
- Orkin saw the Haiti mobile donation program as a step forward in giving, but not something that was directly comparable with the American Cancer Society's funding efforts.

11

Stops and Starts

Hipcricket's Stovall saw several false starts, events that in retrospect could have accelerated mobile's growth but didn't.

"What happened was the BlackBerry came out [in 2003] and the BlackBerry exploded and everybody wanted to get into that business," Stovall says. "So life's great. Everybody is excited about that and we started selling more to brands but still life wasn't good. I was on stage saying, 'This is the year of mobile' and it never was.

"Then three things happened. Google started talking about getting into the wireless space. They threatened to buy Sprint [a wireless carrier in the United States]. Then the iPhone came out [in 2007] and the carriers' network speeds got better. These three things—that was the explosion of mobile marketing."

One of the more confident sellers you will ever find, Hipcricket's Stovall nonetheless describes the early years as choppy.

"It was all over the place," he says. "Today people accept that mobile is here, and they are looking for a solution that will be with them long term. Back then, it always was a trial even if it was yearlong. It was a yearlong trial and people weren't spending big dollars. They were spending conservative dollars."

For Stovall, Orkin, Braiker, and many others, the June 2007 introduction of Apple's iPhone was seen as mobile's defining moment. The iPhone modernized the wireless experience with an intuitive user experience, access to the Web, and applications that met utilitarian needs—the best recipe for cooking a turkey dinner, for instance—and previously unmet desires through the introduction of such popular distractions as an app called Angry Birds and products that gave you the chance to pop more bubbles than your buddy in a 30-second span.

When researcher Joy Liuzzo, vice president and director of InsightExpress, looks at the before and after, she ties parallels to the growth of the Internet.

"When Apple introduced the iPhone back in 2007, it was revolutionary for the mobile industry and for a small subset of early adopters," she says. "In 2007, only 43 percent of people 18 to 24 were texting on a daily basis compared to 70 percent in 2011, and only 8 percent of this same group were using the mobile Internet daily [compared to 42 percent in 2011]. The need for this level of connection was not yet established on a wide basis, and the behaviors were not natural yet.

"Pulling from a past experience, the best way to describe mobile in the early years is to compare it to online adoption. Most people started with America Online like the RAZR phone and got comfortable with the technology and access to information. As more Internet service providers rolled out and Netscape and other browsers were introduced, the early adopters peeled away from AOL and started exploring more functionalities, including early smartphones such as Windows Mobile devices.

"People were outgrowing the limiting experiences of AOL and around that same time, broadband was being introduced through the iPhone and the time to make a move seemed right. As broadband became more widely available, more content was introduced, searching became easier, and the behaviors of usage became more concrete, people left the AOLs in droves."

12

Build Me an iPhone App

IPHONE MANIA STRETCHED ALL the way to C-level suites across corporations worldwide. Marketers who rarely had access to chief executives were summoned to corner offices only to leave with a firm marching order—build us an iPhone app now.

The mandate was largely driven by naïve views that the introduction of an iPhone application would land a company space on the cover of the *Wall Street Journal*. That was proved to be a fallacy as Apple's App Store grew to more than a half million apps and the mere activity of creating an application was for journalists anything but news.

But marketers intent on keeping their jobs charged their in-house and outside teams with app development even if it made no sense. More than one business traveled this unwise path despite the fact that their consumers or prospects were outside of the initial iPhone demographic—young, affluent, and early adopters of technology.

Hipcricket counseled clients to be more strategic, oftentimes to use text messaging for reach because this capability was available on well over 90 percent of handsets. In some cases, it was recommended that brands add on an app to deliver a richer brand experience.

The downside was the app was rarely available in all carrier app stores and could be downloaded only by more robust devices.

Joy Liuzzo of InsightExpress (see Chapter 5) provided similar advice.

"When I first starting talking to brands and agencies back in 2007, my strategy was to educate, educate, educate," she says. "I would speak with them about what consumers were doing on their phones, the trends we were seeing over time, and where we thought the market would be in 6 to 9 months. I would also have a plethora of case studies at the ready to show them what other companies in their category, or a similar category, had done in mobile and the success they had seen. People were interested in running campaigns on mobile, but it was a mental shift for them in executing the campaigns, not nearly as simple as online had become and they were hesitant.

"Companies were making decisions to develop an app and rushing to launch something just so they could point to it in the app store. The lack of strategy is shocking in hindsight—and even during the time—but it spoke to the still naïve understanding of mobile by most companies. They thought of it as an isolated channel, something fun and fluffy, and that consumers would be willing to engage with anything they put in front of them. I think the realization that the channel and consumer were more sophisticated than they realized was a hard wake-up call for brands and agencies. However, those lessons were necessary to force agencies and brands down a more integrated strategy path, one that included proper planning and multiple mobile channel executions and media."

Beyond text messaging, applications, and simple websites, a small but growing minority of brands sought to reach consumers through advertisements on mobile Internet pages and within applications. With no guidelines or established metrics, those who produced mobile ads were figuratively throwing darts to see what would stick.

Although Hipcricket didn't enter this part of the business in a substantial way until 2008, others proceeded with mixed results.

"When InsightExpress first started measuring mobile advertising effectiveness in 2007, the ads we were testing were basic, at best," Liuzzo says. "This worked exceedingly well for companies selling basic things like ringtones, wallpapers, and so on. They didn't need a lot of creative license; they just needed text and bold colors to get their message across. It wasn't great for brands who were out to build aware-ness and drive purchase rather than driving sales on the phone.

"Agencies faced designing creative with a limited color set and very limited size restrictions, all so that the ads could be displayed on the majority of phones. Just getting the logo built into an ad could be a challenge, let alone matching the style guide of the online or TV ads in the campaign. For the video units that were being sold at this time, the sheer amount of compression needed and the physical size of the screen made them very difficult to execute. It wasn't until around 2009 that the ad guidelines allowed for more creativity, more colors, more interaction with the introduction of animated and rich media units. Not so coincidently, this was also the time we saw a significant uptick in the number of smartphones being introduced to the marketplace and more agencies and brands starting to integrate mobile into larger campaigns rather than treating it as a one-off campaign."

13

Hipcricket Matures, Rebrands

LIKE ANY SMALL BUSINESS, especially one in an immature industry, Hipcricket was measured in its hiring and expansion plans. By 2007, Ivan Braiker had seen enough traction that he and the board of directors decided to build out the senior management team and go public on the London Stock Exchange, where Hipcricket's key investors had previously done business. By the summer of that year, I was brought on as chief marketing officer (CMO), Eric Harber joined as president and chief operating officer, and Tom Virgin, a former chief financial officer (CFO) of the year in the small private company category in Seattle, came aboard as CFO.

Ironically, my first meeting with Braiker was also at a Seattle-area coffee shop. I had just left InfoSpace; that company had moved to be the leader in the United States in the delivery of mobile content only to get disintermediated by the carriers and record labels, which demanded more of the margin on goods for themselves.

Beyond Braiker's charisma, I was attracted to Hipcricket for its permission-based mobile programs. To me, the model was fascinating—having a consumer opt in for information and offers rather than spamming them, a technique that personal computer users had become wary of after all the unwanted offers of Viagra and fake Rolex watches.

As a CMO, I saw obvious value in helping Hipcricket's move from the start-up phase and help clients engage with those who raised their hands and said that they wanted to have a relationship with the brand or media company.

Harber, who had been in mobile more than 10 years by the spring of 2007, was equally intrigued.

"In Hipcricket, I saw a small team but a big idea," he says. "They didn't have all the pieces in place but they had the vision of this sort of next evolution—there's another way to reach people and it's this device that's always with them—and it's not with a digital content download. It's with an engagement model.

"In Ivan, I saw someone who was a visionary who had a passion for one industry, primarily the broadcast radio and television industry, and realized that there was an opportunity to take this and embrace other brands and industries."

Harber began his career as an entrepreneur but the years just prior to 2007 were times when he was scaling global businesses.

The contrast was great, Harber thought, but so, too, was the potential.

"This was a teeny, tiny business with a dozen people, but they had interesting customers and they had customers that really liked them," he recalls. "I had been in a lot of businesses in the past—you do your best and the customers, some like you, some don't like you. With that small company, it was sort of the ethos that was developed—serve our customers well. I thought that was pretty impressive. I felt it was something we could build upon. You could build on the idea that customers come first.

"At the time, you had to find people who had an appetite for risk because it was a small company with a big vision. You needed people who could be flexible and could be okay playing the role of educator and evangelist in a market that needed to be matured and needed to be brought along. [Hipcricket employees needed] flexibility, sort of an entrepreneurial spirit, an ability to do more with less. A Swiss Army knife if you will. You could do several different activities, and you could be someone given a task or an area of responsibility to kind of run with it. Raise your hand when you needed help, but otherwise you could go on your own because that's the pace we had to keep."

Virgin, the incoming CFO, too, was wooed and wowed by the personable Braiker.

14

It's Not Spam on the Phone

"I KNEW ALMOST NOTHING about mobile at the time," Tom Virgin remembers. "My first question was, 'Is this a company that is going to spam everyone on their phone?' Of course, it's not—it's all permission-based. I had coffee with Ivan [Braiker]—he interviewed me for five minutes, and then we talked for another hour." By the day's end, Virgin had met with Hipcricket's board chairman.

"It was an indication that they were serious about getting things done and I liked that," Virgin says. "When I joined, I knew they had enough money on the balance sheet to run it for a while. They were working on this IPO [initial public offering]. I figured if nothing else, it would be fun for six months. If there was more to it than that, that was fine."

It turned out to be much more.

"It was casual," Virgin says of his earliest days with Hipcricket. "People were driven to be successful. I felt like people were very passionate about it. We had a mixed bag of people who you could tell were going to be successful and other people who were there and wouldn't stay for too long. I had confidence in the people leading the company."

By fall, Hipcricket was listed on AIM, the London Stock Exchange's international market for smaller growing companies. A wide range of businesses, including early-stage, venture capital–backed, and more established companies, join AIM seeking access to growth capital.

With an infusion of money, Hipcricket sought to quickly grow market share.

"What we realized was that there were a lot of things that we just did over and over again," Virgin says. "Because of the entrepreneurial nature of the people we had, there was not a lot of thought about how to make those things really easy and repeatable—to do them well and as efficiently as possible.

"I remember having discussions about process and that was described as bureaucracy. Eventually I realized that I needed to describe it differently—that we wanted to be efficient and do all the things we did over and over again as well as we could so it would allow us to do the hard things better. Once I convinced the founders that that was what we were really trying to do, not to make it harder to get things done, that worked out well for us."

15

Texting with the Phone to the Ear?

AROUND THE TIME WHEN Hipcricket expanded its senior management ranks, Gay Gabrilska joined the company. She first saw what mobile and Hipcricket could muster when she was a promotions and marketing manager in Dallas at Susquehanna Radio Corporation. She admits during Hipcricket's first demo that she naïvely texted and put the phone to her ear while awaiting a response. But she picked up the platform and Hipcricket advantage early, seeing quick success with a Lasik center that offered a free procedure to a lucky texter who was prompted in a spot. The doctor received 100 leads for a procedure that cost between $7,000 and $8,000.

Gabrilska, now Hipcricket's vice president of mobile solutions, likely was won over by mobile when she saw the power of the medium in the days leading to the landfall of Hurricane Rita. Houston radio station KRBE, part of the Susquehanna Radio Corporation, offered to deliver hurricane alerts via text messaging across cell phones to listeners, enabling information to be delivered regardless of whether a person was near a radio or a computer.

Overnight, KRBE and Hipcricket developed and deployed a custom service that sent in excess of 80,000 messages to Houston residents who opted in to receive hurricane alerts from KRBE.

Programs with public service alerts are now commonplace within Hipcricket's client roster, delivering such vital information as routes away from fires and school closures.

Key Takeaways

- Short message service (SMS), or text, alerts provide recipients with timely, personalized information that affects their lives.
- The ability to set up a campaign in minutes gives mobile marketers nimbleness that their marketing counterparts don't have.
- Given that most mobile subscribers have a text-capable phone, a text campaign is inclusive.

Gabrilska later moved to Seattle to work with Hipcricket and immediately needed her experiences to help silence a skeptical crowd of 30 seasoned radio representatives, managers and sales managers, and interactive people.

"When this person from Hipcricket said that the average age of a texter is 38, the room erupted," Gabrilska tells me. "Everyone just called BS. There was no getting control back of the room and that was on my very first day on the job. I'm sitting there with my phone and I quickly Google the average age of a texter and what pops up is 38. We finally got back some control in the room when I said, 'Whoa, whoa, whoa, whoa, we have eight sources here' and that pretty much calmed everyone down.

"The main instigator in that room came when we were there a year later launching more stations in the radio cluster. He busted into the training and said, 'The last time these people were here I waited six months before I started to listen to what they were saying and believed what it was. Now I'm making more money and people get it and I'm doing right for the client (the advertiser). We're creating engaging radio so stop what you're doing and listen to what they're saying.'"

Gabrilska needed this testimonial and more when the recession began and radio's revenue decline accelerated.

"I never thought that it wouldn't work," she said. "There were moments of frustration but I think we probably all had the time when you came up against a naysayer when you're doing something that is innovative. For some people, it was innovative in 2011."

"I like a good fight. I think you have enough proof and enough direct success stories and you're able to point to people who can help you understand how it is done. You let them talk to someone who knows how it works—that makes it easier. I don't think there was ever one single person that we weren't able to get to come around to our way of thinking."

In the early days, those people included Gus Swanson at Clear Channel Seattle.

"Having radio people associated with Hipcricket allowed us to collaborate on different ideas," Swanson remembers. "When we first involved texting, I was a one-man show for six of these stations and all of the digital assets—websites, e-mail, and subsequently texting. It wasn't a matter of convincing others about the dollars to be spent, it was my nervousness of carving out the time to use the system to its fullest capacity.

"The ability to talk about different scenarios with the Hipcricket staff was a godsend for me because I was able to kind of utilize them as part of my team."

Gabrilska, who over the years hired many of Swanson's Hipcricket account managers, describes the work environment this way:

"It's really different but similar to radio in that it is really intense, there's a lot going on, but you have people who are really type A and will take on more than the average person would driven by a passion and driven by not proving someone wrong, but proving someone right."

Several milestones showed Hipcricket that it was doing more than a few things right.

In 2007, Hipcricket received the first of what would be unprecedented back-to-back pioneer awards presented by CTIA–The Wireless Association. This followed an industry-leading 300 percent increase in the use of short codes for text messaging programs.

"Hipcricket realized the power and potential ubiquity of CSCs [common short codes] early on, and they've made believers of broadcasters and brands alike," says Diane Strahan, then vice president of mobile at Neustar, the entity that registers short codes on behalf of CTIA and the mobile operators. "Hipcricket has significantly advanced the popularity and exposure of this fantastic mobile marketing vehicle, and they are richly deserving of recognition."

The year 2008 was equally as noteworthy. In the spring, Hipcricket launched the industry's first Hispanic mobile marketing network. For decades, brand marketers have sought the most effective ways to reach Hispanic consumers, whose buying power exceeds $1 trillion, according to the Selig Center for Economic Growth at the University of Georgia's Terry College of Business.

Knowing that mobile provides an ideal conduit to Hispanics, who are among the most active users of mobile technology and text messaging, Hipcricket developed a mobile marketing and advertising network to enable marketers to reach opted-in Hispanic mobile subscribers. Unlike discrete databases built individually by brands and broadcasters, the network aggregated Hispanics who gave Hipcricket broadcast clients permission to reach them with offers and information from multiple brands.

Through the network, clients including HBO, Arby's, and Harley-Davidson ran programs to reach more than 7 million Hispanic radio listeners in the leading markets across the country such as Los Angeles, Miami, Chicago, and New York.

Hipcricket chose to build the Hispanic-focused network due to that group's high interest in mobile devices and marketing. In a 2008 Mobile Marketing Association (MMA) study, 32 percent of Hispanic consumers indicated that they were moderately or highly receptive to mobile marketing messages. At that time, 75 percent of all U.S. Hispanic households had multiple mobile phones and used them more than any other form of personal technology. More than half regularly used text messaging, according to MMA data.

It was in part because of that development that the analyst firm Frost & Sullivan later in 2008 called Hipcricket "the early leader" in the United States in mobile marketing.

"Hipcricket is a clear market leader within its target segment," said Vikrant Gandhi, senior analyst, mobile and wireless, Frost & Sullivan. "The company successfully leverages its technical expertise and experience to develop and deliver highly customized, turnkey mobile marketing campaigns. Continually innovating and differentiating its offerings, Hipcricket has also shown a tremendous ability to identify lucrative market segments—such as Hispanic Americans—and then deliver solutions tailored specifically to helping advertisers reach these targets."

According to Frost & Sullivan, "Hipcricket's success can be attributed to a mix of smart leadership, effective sales strategy, and technical expertise. Hipcricket's management has extensive experience in the radio and television markets, which helps the company truly understand the strategic imperatives of its key customers and design effective solutions to help them maximize the mobile marketing potential."

Further, "The company has one of the fastest turnarounds in the industry—Hipcricket's team turns creative briefs into executable programs in 48 hours or less by leveraging the extensive in-house database of information about thousands of mobile marketing campaigns managed previously."

Hipcricket was among the earliest mobile marketing companies to advocate for cross-media integration, undoubtedly in part because the firm's roots were in traditional media.

16

Mobile Award *For Dummies*

To CAP 2008, THE Mobile Marketing Association presented Hipcricket with the North America Cross-Media Integration award for work done with Wiley Publishing around the *For Dummies* franchise.

Complementing marketing spends in e-mail, online college newsletters, and out-of-home ads, Wiley and Hipcricket promoted the annual Dummies Month during March with texting, mobile advertising, and a mobile website intended to reach women ages 18 to 34, who are the primary purchasers of *For Dummies* titles.

The campaign's objectives included driving awareness of the monthly promotion and $5 rebate offer, encouraging consumers to visit local retail stores to purchase *For Dummies* titles, and engaging consumers at the point of sale using mobile calls to action on posters and flyers.

The mobile marketing promotion of Dummies Month included a text-to-win sweepstakes to win high-end consumer electronics prizes via short message service (SMS), using the keyword *Dummies* to reinforce Wiley's *Dummies* brand. Once consumers texted-in *Dummies* to a common short code, their e-mail address was captured and they were sent a rebate for $5 off any Wiley *For Dummies* title.

41

Hipcricket designed and ran mobile banner ads across a number of mobile websites to extend the program's reach to millions of wireless data subscribers. The Dummies mobile website, also designed and developed by Hipcricket, supported the campaign and offered consumers an easy way to opt in to receive those offers and rebates via e-mail. An important element of the site was the store locator, which enabled users to enter their zip code to find the closest store that carried the *For Dummies* titles—helping to drive in-store retail traffic.

The mobile site also included a list of the most popular *For Dummies* titles. In addition, the site allowed users to enter their mobile phone numbers to sign up for the For Dummies Club, which would push regular updates to these consumers.

The TXT4Dummies campaign met its objectives, drawing more than 1.3 million impressions—330,000 more than planned. The mobile advertisements resulted in an average click-through rate of 1.4 percent, four times the click-through rate of similar online ads, according to Juston Payne, then manager of online advertising at John Wiley & Sons.

"We saw significantly higher engagement with mobile ads than we ever did with Internet banner ads," Payne says.

Key Takeaways

- Because the offer was the same, the campaign provided the brand with an accurate way of gauging mobile behavior versus online behavior.
- SMS was not the end-all for the brand manager who wanted a richer experience via mobile.
- There were multiple calls to action, ensuring that consumers would see the offer whether they were in store, online, or on a mobile device.

With a recession under way and mobile fighting every day for reduced marketing budgets, Eric Harber had little time in late 2008 to reflect on the early days or the year's accomplishments. He looks back now with lessons learned.

"I think it was pretty difficult," he says. "That evangelist role in [the] '07 and '08 time frame, not that we still don't do that today, you were literally on a sales call describing to someone how to use the mobile device for something other than making a phone call.

"Text or SMS was the second most popular activity on the phone at that time and you were on a sales call with a very savvy marketer or CMO [chief marketing officer] and you had to literally help them get their phone out and be able to send or receive a text message. That was kind of the state of the nation at the time. Even if they had the fanciest phone at the time, they didn't understand all that they could do with it and all a marketer could do to use that as a conduit to their customers and prospects."

That was about to change as 2009 began.

PART II

The Present

MOBILE CLAWS ITS WAY into marketing budgets with returns on investment—everything from more sales to brand loyalty.

17

The Recession's Effect on Mobile's Growth

Businesses, Especially Retail, Feel the Pinch

It was more life-changing for those who lost their homes and jobs, but the deepest recession to hit the global economy since the Great Depression brought large challenges to many marketers. Business was off across the board, and the relatively few dollars that consumers had accumulated remained in their pockets alongside those feature phones and smartphones.

The retail industry was among the most affected, with stores regularly going out of business and landlords facing a difficult, if not impossible, time filling an overabundance of empty spaces.

Coinciding with the worst of the economic woes was the increased adoption of mobile devices. Yes, the prices for phones were high (although not as high as they were for the DynaTAC or StarTAC) and the carriers required multiyear contracts for the best deals, but consumers bought in unprecedented numbers. In fact, the number of mobile subscribers in the United States had grown to 322 million by June 2011, up by more than 100 million over a five-year period, according to CTIA–The Wireless Association.

Simon Shops for Visitors

The job of driving shoppers to the mall and to engage with them while they are there falls to retail marketers like Patrick Flanagan, vice president of digital strategy at Simon Property Group.

Approximately 100 million unique shoppers annually flow through Simon's 400 malls, according to the company. Given where consumer behavior has moved, what better way to reach out to them than via their most personal devices—the cell phone they carried all day and slept near all night?

"We see the breadth and width of America from every consumer segment you can think of," Flanagan says. "One of the few common things that everyone has at this point is mobile. It's the absolute focus of the CEO [chief executive officer] on down to use all things mobile to connect to these shoppers, to market to these shoppers with offers or to get feedback from these shoppers, and to deliver content. Really any use case, if there isn't a mobile component, it doesn't meet our stated strategic sniff test."

When Flanagan arrived at the largest real estate company in the United States after a decade-long career in digital marketing, the company had what he says was an "out of date" mobile website that had nothing more than a store-finder feature and functionality to provide gift card balances. Those features were certainly more than what many offered, but Flanagan lamented the fact that there were no mobile applications, no text messaging program, and no database built of VIP shoppers who might have elected to receive information and offers from Simon and its retailers.

Flanagan says that although Simon management didn't know the *how*, it knew that a larger investment in mobile would make a difference.

"They didn't know the details," Flanagan recalls. "They probably didn't even understand the downside risk but they knew directionally that we had to go that way. For other folks like me and my team, we figured out the good vendors and partners along the way to help us. But it was [from senior management], 'Don't miss the bus. Get on. I'll trust you guys not to screw it up.'"

Time to Get Personal

Smack in the middle of the recession, Flanagan eyed a more personal relationship with Simon shoppers, one that would figuratively drive consumers to his malls rather than someone else's properties—or, worse yet, to no one's.

"The business problem we have is how do you differentiate yourself as a mall," Flanagan explains. "You can ask shoppers what they care about—why do they go to any particular mall?

"The first answer is distance. Well, you can't really move a mall. The second one is the mix of stores—that's a long-term and challenging thing to change. The third one is the customer experience—it had better parking, it had free Wi-Fi, it had a better food court or cleaner bathrooms. Mobile is where we think we can ultimately differentiate as a business."

Text Programs to Be Inclusive

Flanagan chose to employ Hipcricket in part to be able to communicate with customers regardless of the type of phone they were carrying. With more than 95 percent of phones in use having a short message service (SMS) or text messaging capability, Simon started with calls to actions that could be seen in malls and in the company's mass marketing materials.

From there, he asked those who had responded if they wanted to join local VIP clubs where they would interact with the mall and its stores in exchange for information and offers.

"Text continues to be our fastest channel on mobile," he says. "It's also our widest reach and is by far adopted by more of our actual people in our malls. Unlike other brands that run one Facebook page, one Twitter stream, one text club, we run 200 of everything—200 unique text clubs is how we set it up in the Hipcricket system. It's how we think about it.

"Each local mall has a unique set of [database] subscribers who are looking for local content. For us, that was the most important thing. That the [Simon] people at the local malls could actually be creating the messages, creating the content, and figuring out what would be enough to not bug someone on their mobile phone and to have the feeling that they actually have some value from it so they wouldn't opt out. We have literally hundreds [of Simon employees]—I don't even know how many—who can order up a text message [campaign].

Getting them comfortable with this was much easier. They could get their heads around it quickly.

'Oh, yeah, it's like a mini-e-mail.'

'Well, give or take, no formatting and no images but you could send your message to your mall shoppers.'

'Oh, great.'"

Value Perceived Despite Inexact Measurement

Beyond consumers, Simon believes that it is providing great benefits to its customers—the retailers who lease space.

Says Flanagan: "It is challenging to have a closed-loop feedback system from someone receiving an offer on a text message that may not have a coupon code or something unique or a trackable hook to be able to report back to the retailer and say, 'Hey, I had 36 incremental sales that came off of my push-based text.' We don't do that and very few retailers have worked that out. That's a place we're looking to get into.

"[Instead the result is that] we sent it to the club. It's a softer measurement. Your landlord is actually pushing sales to you. Right off the bat they say, 'This is great. Usually you're just trying to take money from me.' It helps shift what sometimes could be a challenging relationship to be more of a collaborative partnership. 'Your sales suck. You're going to go out of business or ask for rent relief.'

"It's in both of our interests to get a lot of people into the mall and a lot of people into the stores. We both win in that. It's free for them to access at this point. The downside is minimal. It's, heck, let's put out an offer and see what we can get."

Key Takeaways

- Training is key because Simon Malls has empowered individual locations to create local mobile campaigns.
- Communications with retail tenants is important so the retailers know what to do when a shopper brings a mobile deal into the store.
- Simon Malls won't wait until the metrics are perfect—it needs to reach consumers on their mobile devices today.

18

Behavior Changes Seen in All Age Groups

BY 2009, THOSE TOO stubborn to look at the numbers continued to make the claim that only those 45 years old and younger were using mobile phones. The statistics clearly told a different story.

In a study conducted early that year by the marketing research company InsightExpress, 84 percent of younger American Boomers (ages 45 to 54) and 79 percent of older American Boomers (ages 55 to 64) owned cell phones. In fact, wireless had become the technology of choice for many younger Boomers, with only 65 percent using a personal computer at the time to access the Internet.

Delving further, smartphone penetration had reached only 17 percent, with Generation Y (ages 18 to 24) choosing the most sophisticated devices one out of every four purchases, followed closely by Generation X (ages 25 to 44) at 24 percent.

The younger the mobile user, the more likely he or she was to rely on the phone for current information, use the device more than a computer to reach the Web, and have an interest in making a purchase with a single click.

Overall, 1 in 10 were interested in signing up for text alerts. About the same number of mobile subscribers had used a social networking service via mobile, with Facebook leading the way followed by soon-to-be-fading MySpace.

Among the most interesting findings surrounded the Generation Y mobile subscriber. InsightExpress found that mobile was being used as a "social crutch," with 38 percent admitting to having pretended to use their phone when no one was on the other end and 34 percent having arranged to have someone call their mobile to "rescue them" from an uncomfortable situation.

Also, the 18- to 24-year-olds were looking at their phones as a "boredom fighter," with 56 percent saying that they used their devices to look for new things. Finally, and not overly surprising, this group used mobile for "instant gratification." According to the research, 47 percent had sent a text message that they later regretted.

Taking a larger view as well, InsightExpress divided wireless subscribers into three groups—the Mobile Pioneer, the Mobile Wannabe, and the Mobile Traditionalist.

The company said at the time 15 percent were Mobile Pioneers, distinguished by their interest in using advanced features like the Web, applications, and video weekly. The majority were younger than 35 years old, one-third had a smartphone, and they were more likely to be male, single, and a minority.

Twenty-five percent fit the description of Mobile Wannabe. They had tried advanced features but were not regular users. Less than half of people in this category were younger than 35, and only 5 percent owned a smartphone.

The remaining 60 percent were Mobile Traditionalists, content to use mobile just for phone calls and texting. Two-thirds of this group were older than 35 years old. Significantly, texting had evolved into an activity on an equal footing with the more traditional phone-calling function of mobile.

Of most interest to mobile marketers, 38 percent of Mobile Pioneers had participated in a contest via text message, compared with 18 percent of Mobile Wannabes and 8 percent of Mobile Traditionalists.

"I first noticed a shift in conversations around the second half of 2009," says Joy Liuzzo, InsightExpress vice president and director.

"Folks were coming to me with questions around mobile advertising and marketing tactics rather than curiosity about the mobile consumer. The tactical conversations focused on simple things like banners until sometime in 2010, when rich media became a larger part of the discussion.

"For our clients, metrics were always important, even if they weren't ready to do mobile yet. Oftentimes the availability of metrics was what encouraged our clients to dip their toe into mobile. They knew they could compare mobile performance to their other media, providing executives with clear ROI [return on investment] and hopefully getting a larger budget for future campaigns. As the campaign budgets grew, we encouraged clients to expand their understanding by conducting cross media studies to look at the synergistic impact of all their media, including mobile."

19

Mobile Gets Busy

The Rise of the Call to Action

34 Cars Sold after None Moved in More Than One Month

Like the retail space and the housing market, the automotive industry also suffered in the throes of the economic quagmire. In 2009 few were driven to think car buying, resulting in woeful sales numbers, the loss of tens of millions of jobs, and the shutdown of dealerships across America.

As it was around the country, the situation was grim near the nation's capital. How dire? Well, one Chevrolet dealer in Timonium, Maryland, had failed to sell even one car during a period lasting more than a month.

Rather than stop spending in marketing, in the spring of that year, Fox Chevrolet turned to Hipcricket client Hearst Baltimore to get creative—something the U.S. government would finally do later that year with a Cash for Clunkers economy stimulator that was designed to rescue auto sellers.

The radio-combined-with-mobile program worked like this: Fox Chevrolet bought two weeks of airtime on Hearst's 98 Rock radio station to run 10- and 15-second promotions encouraging listeners to text in to enter to win the chance to purchase a car for $98.

In total, nearly 500 listeners texted the keyword *Fox* to the station's short code. Each was entered to win and given details on how to attend the drawing at Fox.

On a Saturday morning, nearly 300 showed up on the lot and two were given the opportunity to purchase a car for $98.

Although the foot traffic was nice, it doesn't begin to measure the success of the campaign. With prospective buyers enticed by shiny cars and competitive deals, Fox turned around its fortunes by selling 17 new cars and 17 used cars at full price on that one day.

20

Radio Regains Its Magic

HUGUES JEAN, HEARST RADIO Baltimore's general sales manager, had envisioned successes such as its text-in contest ever since he was sold on mobile and Hipcricket in 2006.

"There is something very unique about radio," he says. "We know we are probably the only medium [reaching consumers] in drive time. What was very interesting with this advertiser was that they were reminding folks about their cars while they were sitting in the middle of traffic. They were targeting drivers in drive time, morning and afternoon drive, and you had to RSVP.

"In this area, we have one of the longest commute times, lot of traffic. We took advantage of that with radio and mobile and the concept itself. On the day of event, we used a push element—sending text messages to remind people to show up. The results were a very, very successful day for this car dealer."

The results were arguably even more impressive than the 680,000 cars that were sold at a reduced price during the government-subsidized Cash for Clunkers program.

Key Takeaways

- A radio promotion was the ideal vehicle for an auto dealer aiming to reach prospective buyers in drive time.
- The dealer's aim was to bring prospects to the car lot—300 was a large number and great return on investment (ROI) given the cost of the radio spot.
- This program proved that mobile could provide ROI even in a recession.

21

Hipcricket Weathers the Recession

ALTHOUGH THEY DIDN'T ALWAYS grab the headlines, such successes as the one seen in Baltimore were common for Ivan Braiker and his Hipcricket colleagues. By 2009, Hipcricket ran compelling demonstrations with mobile phones, injected the measurability-of-mobile story into its sales materials and pitches, and gave jittery marketers and advertisers confidence that their dollars would be more trackable and work harder when used in conjunction with calls to action inserted into media that they were already employing.

As a result, Hipcricket became the go-to mobile provider for broadcast companies with increased business from Clear Channel among others. Hipcricket also saw a pickup in assignments from brands and agencies, in large part because it had moved to become a full-service company that could bring clients broad and deep offerings that ran from strategy to a gamut of products and services, including mobile advertising, mobile Web, and analytics.

The business advanced but Tom Virgin, Hipcricket's chief financial officer, was in search of even more traction.

"I think I was frustrated because every year has been the 'Year of Mobile' since we got here," he says. "I think we're still waiting for the 'Year of Mobile' but it's looking better. It was frustrating for a while, then we figured out it was the same for everybody in mobile, and, in fact, because of the downturn in the economy, it was the same for a lot of people in a lot of companies. We used that time to take care of a lot of things within the company so it wasn't like we weren't making things better for ourselves."

One of those things was to step up marketing to differentiate Hipcricket from the many newcomers who were opening for business even in the recession's darkest days.

"The broadcasters who were getting it were getting it," Braiker says. "There was still a hesitancy from the ones who didn't get it—we even see that today. You also had the long tail [mobile marketing] groups—the three guys in the garage who would try and go sell these radio stations essentially nothing more than a rebound system. A rebound system is not mobile marketing."

By licensing a rebound system, all the stations were able to do was to send a response back if someone texted in. Those who took that route had not contracted for a robust, easy-to-use platform like Hipcricket's, preventing those stations from building mobile VIP clubs and marketing to an opted-in database of listeners who had raised their hands and said that they wanted to interact with the station and its advertisers.

"A picture is a thousand words," Braiker says. "Being able to demonstrate what we do and let somebody see it on my phone is valuable. All of a sudden, the gears kick right in—you can just hear them. Instead of us saying text-in the word and you get this back, when you can see the chain that happens and you can demonstrate that on a phone or you can demonstrate something on a mobile website, and show how easy it is to make this happen . . . it's the most powerful device ever created by man and it's going to continue to be that."

More Radio Success

Clear Channel Cleveland

Those stations that had employed the complete solution experienced both sales and programming benefits. In fact, in Cleveland, Clear Channel's

Kris Foley says that she was able to bring in an additional $1 million in advertising revenue in eight months by including a mobile component.

"We actually took the approach of holding seminars where we would invite three or four clients, not competing businesses, and talk to them about new technology that we were embracing," she says. "We were positioned as innovative and that is so important in marketing. I firmly believe if you're not moving forward, then you're going to be moving quickly behind. These meetings were very informative for clients. A lot of them were still hesitant to jump in because it was something new."

Not surprisingly, the campaigns that received the most listener response were those that included discounts for products and services.

"The biggest problem we had was around mobile coupons," Foley says. "People were concerned that, 'Oh, what if someone forwards them along? What if someone tries to hijack the system?' It doesn't happen. 'What if I don't train my employees and the customer has a bad experience?'

"All of those things have very easy answers if you just think about them in advance and have a plan for them. If someone was to forward a text along with an offer, isn't that a wonderful thing because they obviously think the next person they send it to will want to respond? Training your employees for better customer service to respond to these coupons—isn't that also a wonderful thing that they're going to step up the level of service with the end user?"

Foley grew her business from station sponsors through conservative pricing and by presenting case studies backed with results.

"We did these seminars, included it [texting] in programming, and made raving fans," she says. "The way you make raving fans is they tell their friends and those in their networks and you start to grow and you prove that they want to work with the station. You prove it by saying, 'I had 300 people in an open house last week.' Then when you have a successful platform, you can bring in the fees."

Hearst Baltimore; Clear Channel Detroit and Seattle; Ramar in Lubbock, Texas

In Baltimore, Hearst's Hugues Jean was not only watching an evolution but creating one.

"The minute I heard about texting in the trade [industry], I felt that we had found a very, very powerful tool of communication that was going to be here to stay," he recalls. "I remember the first day we went on the air and told our listeners that we had a short code—56332. We had 1,200 texts the same day. From that point, I realized there was an opportunity for us to create and generate new revenue with a new medium.

"We took this opportunity right away to advertisers because for me, I knew it was measurable. We knew we could prove that radio is really working. It was very challenging in the beginning because texting was fairly new to advertisers. They had this perception that it was a very, very young listener texting all the time. [Having an advertiser] paying $2,500 or $3,500 for a campaign was very challenging. But the minute we did it, we realized that they were creating events at their locations, they were getting tangible results, listeners were showing up at events, and we had the data to support what we were saying. We used half a dozen success stories or testimonials at the beginning and kept running with it."

Among the early adopters was the American Red Cross, which had been spending with Hearst Baltimore for more than a quarter century.

"We have been doing mega-drives every year for the American Red Cross for the past 26 years," Jean says. "In fact, it's the largest single blood drive in Maryland. When we started a texting program, they were convinced that it was very powerful for them using the push element to remind listeners that, 'Today is the blood drive, don't forget to stop by the locations and save lives.'"

The American Red Cross also used mobile and radio in Detroit. During a monthlong campaign run on two Clear Channel stations, the organization addressed an awareness issue around the urgent need for blood donors by becoming the stations' text title sponsor. It was able to send more than 15,000 messages to those who had texted the stations with song requests and comments.

"I've always been open to more efficient ways to market to our listeners," says Clint Buckingham, director of digital content, Clear Channel Detroit. "I started in radio in a studio taking listener calls and witnessed firsthand, and was part of, the move into the digital realm. This is a complementary step."

Meanwhile, while not exactly saving lives, Gus Swanson of Clear Channel Seattle was making raving fans by being first in delivering sports information to on-the-go listeners of sports station 950 KJR. He built a relatively large VIP club and took steps to be relevant to each listener by capturing specific interests during the sign-up process.

For instance, during a period when the National Basketball Association's Sonics were in court trying to move to Oklahoma City, his disc jockeys encouraged listeners to opt in to receive Sonics-related news. Listeners who chose to do so were sent updates during the trial as well as the final disappointing outcome that the basketball team was leaving. In only 30 days, the station expanded the Sonics portion of its database by 562 percent over the previous year.

"It's still tolerance," Swanson says. "It's the listener who asked for that particular bit of information that we're able to push to them."

Key Takeaways

- As ESPN executives explain elsewhere in this book, sports are personal—Swanson wisely gave fans only the information that mattered to them.
- The judge's decision was on the minds of many in Seattle—there was no more immediate way to receive the news than via a mobile alert.
- KJR served its tribe, offering those who could not listen to the station at the time to be in the know and receive the news from the people they trust.

In Lubbock, Texas, Chris Fleming, chief revenue officer and radio general manager for Ramar Communications, sends approximately 30,000 messages a month to those who have opted in to receive local weather. The program grows by approximately 2,000 people a month, according to Fleming.

Jiffy Lube Tracks New Customers

John Wanamaker, considered by some to be the so-called father of advertising, once asserted that the problem with the discipline is that although 50 percent works, no one knows which 50 percent.

Mobile doesn't entirely answer the question of what half of advertising works, but it allows marketers and business owners to make better assumptions.

Consider the case of Ames, Iowa–based KCCQ and a local Jiffy Lube location.

To sell more spots and to differentiate itself from the competition, the radio station turned to Hipcricket and mobile to provide additional measurability to advertising campaigns. Jiffy Lube's interests were twofold: (1) acquire new customers, in part by adding a mobile component to traditional radio ads, and (2) have existing customers return for more service.

Here's how the campaign worked:

KCCQ and Jiffy Lube gave listeners the chance to win free oil changes for a year. Each listener who entered the contest received a coupon via text message that included discounts on oil changes, wiper blades, tire rotations, and filters.

Tracking redemption gave the parties data that radio spots previously could not deliver.

"Roughly 50 percent of the respondents have been from new households, and our other advertising methods bring in 20 percent at most," says Andrew Storjohann, general manager of the local Jiffy Lube facility. "This is based on the tractable text coupons and doesn't even take into account what the radio commercials create on their own."

Key Takeaways

- This campaign showed that there are inexpensive and simple ways to measure traditional media campaigns.
- Providing consumers the ability to receive an offer via text message allowed for the largest mobile reach possible.
- Jiffy Lube had greater insight that it could factor in to its subsequent marketing spend.

Tom Joyner Converts a Monologue into a Dialogue

Before the days of mobile, Tom Joyner built a radio empire by talking with his audience rather than to it. The Tom Joyner Morning Show and BlackAmericaWeb.com reach more than 8 million African American adult consumers each week in an environment that builds community.

A mobile component, begun in 2008, adds to the closeness Joyner feels with his listeners.

"We know that as these loyal consumers listen to our programming, most of them are in transit, so we wanted to give our listeners the opportunity to have immediate and impactful communication directly with Tom and the crew," says Julia Atherton, executive vice president of Reach Media, which was founded by Joyner. "The mobile platform has allowed us to convert a monologue into a dialogue with our listeners.

"The responses and feedback that we get each morning allow us to generate immediate customization of our programming for our listeners. Within minutes of airing a segment on the *Tom Joyner Morning Show*, we will get mobile messages from our listeners adding their two cents. This feedback is priceless as we program the show and the corresponding digital elements."

One early lesson was the need for authenticity.

"We believe in superserving the African American community," Atherton says. "Knowing that our audience is very technologically savvy and prides itself on being early adopters, this new communication tool was a natural fit for the *Tom Joyner Morning Show*.

"We learned very quickly that our outgoing messages to the Text Tom Club members needed to come from Tom's voice and point of view. Any messages that were construed as being overly commercial and not in harmony with our brand essence were disregarded."

Each message receives personal attention.

"We also reminded ourselves of the lessons we all learned from following the Golden Rule," she says. "When someone takes the time and effort to send us a message, we respond. This isn't a typical 'bounce back' message. We have paid staff who are responsible for responding to each text message and printing out copies for Tom to read. Any messages that require action are then forwarded to the appropriate person within our company. It is a huge commitment, but we truly believe that you should 'do unto others.'

"We measure success by using the immediate communication from our listeners into the programming content of the *Tom Joyner Morning Show* and BlackAmericaWeb.com. At the end of the day, we are in the communication industry. A mobile platform offers our listeners a convenient and cost-efficient method to 'talk' to Tom and our organization. The immediacy strengthens our brand image, which translates into ratings and revenue."

22

The Brands Rebound
from the Recession

MEANWHILE, MOBILE HAD BECOME of greater interest to brand marketers as well as the agencies that service them, be they advertising, promotional, or public relations firms.

Attesting to mobile marketing's traction and Hipcricket's leadership with such clients as Nestlé, HBO, and Arby's, the company doubled its total campaign count in 2009 and surpassed 50,000.

Hipcricket further teamed with major brands and media to create and run integrated mobile programs that led to permission-based databases with member counts well into the six figures. The company saw significant response for mobile coupons and offers that led to trials and sales. In response, it introduced a measureable solution that placed mobile coupons within reach of the then more than 240 million Americans who had text messaging on their mobile phones.

Based on patent-pending technology, the new mobile coupon solution enabled any business with a point of sale system that accepted credit cards to fully track and measure the redemption and usage patterns of mobile coupons to increase customer loyalty and sales.

Selling on the Fear Factor

Doug Stovall, Hipcricket's senior vice president of sales and client services, explains the brand marketer's use of mobile in 2009 this way:

"The Internet happened 10 years ago and you had a lot of companies and marketers that missed it. And they are so terrified of missing the next one—and right now they are getting hit with the next one constantly. Mobile. Facebook. The social phenomenon. Every marketer is going to get out there for the sake of his or her job. That's why they're doing mobile.

"In 2009, it was the fear factor. We sold on the fear factor and it wasn't about being aggressive. It was saying, 'Mobile is here, do you want to try something?' Everyone was willing to try something because mobile is less expensive. That fear turned into small projects which then proved out mobile. The recession left, mobile was being proven out, the devices were getting better, coverage was getting better and faster, and now we're in the explosion. We have three to five years of explosion, maybe more."

Engaging the Brands

The selling of the virtues of mobile marketing wasn't easy for anyone, including Joy Liuzzo of InsightExpress, and Thom Kennon, the former digital lead at WPP agency Wunderman and now senior vice president and director of strategy for sister agency Y&R.

"We found ourselves in the position of 'hype busters,'" says Liuzzo. "Mobile was the bright shiny new object and sometimes the excitement got in the way of proper strategy. I would have meetings where people were focused on building an app as a branding strategy and realize during the meeting that their target market wasn't using smartphones. Other meetings would be focused on getting consumers to sign up for text alerts, only the client didn't have a strategy for future communications.

"We discovered that the need for education didn't stop once mobile became part of the media mix. If anything, it became a more integral component to avoid campaign failures. The educational conversations started turning toward more tactical conversations around mid-2009 and that was a pleasant change. Rather than giving people information to justify testing mobile campaigns, we were discussing the targeting options, the mix of media—banners, rich media, and so on—and the success metrics."

Kennon, who is also an adjunct professor at New York University teaching graduate students integrated marketing, saw himself educating professional marketers as well.

"One of the jobs I've taken on in the States, either with my work with the MMA [Mobile Marketing Association] or the agency or in my teaching is to convince folks that mobile isn't just a nice to have, it's not just an add on, it's not just the next shiny thing on the shelf," he says. "It can and should be the centerpiece of their all-channel advertising and marketing.

"My experience so far has been in fits and starts in getting brands to add mobile in any significant way to the mix beyond just a quirky nice-to-have [for example] 'Let's do an iPhone app.' That's not a strategy. It suffers from the same flaw of the conversation of three or four or five years ago from those who said, 'Let's have a Facebook page. Let's drive Fans and Likes.' It's not a strategy. It's a tactic."

23

The Rise of Loyalty Clubs

FROM HIS FIRST HIPCRICKET-RELATED meeting in Starbucks in 2004, Ivan Braiker preached the benefits of asking consumers for permission to market to them. He knew then that those who would choose to interact with brands or broadcast stations would receive great value in the relationship and likely buy more stuff from the advertiser or listen more to the station.

By 2009, growing consumer interest in mobile marketing and customer loyalty programs had created a significant and largely untapped opportunity for brands to connect with customers on their mobile devices. The second annual Hipcricket Mobile Marketing Survey showed that whereas 37 percent of consumers would be interested in participating in a mobile customer loyalty program from a brand that they trust, 83 percent said that their favorite brand had yet to market to them via their most personal device—their mobile phone.

Further, the study showed that mobile marketing campaigns were becoming significantly more influential and effective. Hipcricket found that of those consumers who had received mobile marketing offers, 47 percent had brand recall and 94 percent of those remembered the specific call to action.

Up until that point, arguably no one had fully taken advantage of the opportunity to engage, then reengage, with consumers. And then Arby's turned to Jimmy Kimmel.

Arby's Goes Mobile Late-Night

Some, probably many, may have had too good a time to remember, but a great deal of us among the 95 million who watched the Super Bowl in February 2009 remember the television spots run by restaurant chain Denny's to promote free Grand Slam breakfasts. The campaign's elements were easy to follow—all viewers needed to do was to go to a Denny's the following Tuesday for free eggs along with toast and hash browns or grits.

Denny's reported that approximately 2 million took advantage of the offer. Although many might view that as a success, Denny's was left with egg on its face when quick-service restaurant Arby's did it one better two months later by building in a way to remarket to patrons through a high-profile, national television campaign.

Here's how it worked:

To start out, for the launch of its Roastburger product, Arby's and Hipcricket had comedian/entertainer Jimmy Kimmel create, eat, and promote the new sandwich on *Jimmy Kimmel Live*, a late-night nationally broadcast TV program airing on ABC.

Viewers were urged to text the word *Roastburger* 27297 to receive a free sandwich with the purchase of any drink. After texting, customers were asked to respond with their zip code to be entered into a local database and to receive additional offers from Arby's. By doing this, the restaurant gained a valuable remarketable database.
As a result of the one segment:

- Arby's received 177,745 total entries from 152,280 unique participants.
- Approximately 65,000 people opted in to join the mobile loyalty club.
- The restaurant created 172 local databases to cater to the opted-in customers on a hyperlocal level.

Hooked on integrating mobile into traditional buys, the restaurant chain brought prominent calls to action into additional TV and radio commercials, print ads, and Sunday coupon circulars and promoted its short codes at live events, including Cavaliers NBA games in Cleveland and a Jonas Brothers concert in Tulsa, Oklahoma, and on in-store signage.

By using different keywords for each channel, Arby's has been able to track the success of each medium. Specifically:

- By later in the year, in-store signage had resulted in more than 41,000 people beginning text interaction; of those customers, more than 89 percent had opted in to join a local database.
- TV promotions outside of the Kimmel program resulted in more than 35,000 people beginning text interaction; of those, more than 90 percent had opted in to join a local database.

Based on the success on *Jimmy Kimmel Live*, Arby's launched a second national TV campaign to promote the restaurant's Fruitea products. Customers were prompted to text the word *Fruitea* to 27297 to receive a free Fruitea beverage with the purchase of any sandwich. This campaign resulted in 16,266 total entries from 15,307 unique participants.

The prominence of Arby's text-based calls to action across all advertising channels was an industry first for mobile marketing. Prior to these campaigns, mobile calls to action had primarily been hidden at the bottom of the screen or page or added as an afterthought. By making mobile the center of its campaigns, Arby's achieved spectacular, even unmatched, results.

"It's awfully nice to have a great call to action on national television," says Hipcricket chief operating officer Eric Harber. "It was some of the early stages of local mobile. We were able to create different segments based on location. Arby's saw the power and beauty of speaking to their different segmentation groups and we were big proponents of that. It was great to see a large brand embrace our idea of local mobile and segmentation.

"It was a success for Arby's and, for Hipcricket, I think it was super helpful. We had the ability to show something with a high profile— how to make it mobile and interactive. It was right out of our strategy and playbook to take advantage of our technology."

Key Takeaways

- Arby's use of a celebrity brought heightened attention to the mobile component of the product launch.
- The creation of loyal databases enabled Arby's to provide relevant offers—it knew to offer iced tea discounts in January to California customers and not to those who were still trying to remove the chill from a Boston Nor'easter storm.
- Calls to action on additional media made those dollars work harder.

24

MillerCoors Drinks from Android Cup

LIKE ARBY'S, MILLERCOORS EMPLOYED short message service (SMS) at first while preparing for the day when smartphone penetration would justify broader programs to include such tactics as applications, the mobile Web, and even geo-fencing, which uses technology to reach opted-in mobile subscribers in a designated local area.

"It was probably 2008, mobile was very much a text-driven world, which is great," says Steve Mura, director of digital marketing at MillerCoors. "It still is very much a text-driven world. Text programs were cheaper, they were more consumer-friendly and easily understood from the retailer perspective. It just made this world we live in easier to navigate for everyone—consumers, companies, and retailers.

"There was this waiting period. We said text was great and it's working but what's next? Then you started to see GPS [Global Positioning Systems] pop up on phones, and that became interesting and then obviously the big game changer was the iPhone. It wasn't a big game changer for the masses but it was a game change and sort of woke up the beast and then everyone said, 'Smartphones are it.

They're the next thing—look at all the things these mini-computers in your hands can do,' and then everyone saw the potential."

But it wasn't the iPhone and Apple's closed iOS operating system but another operating system that MillerCoors needed.

"The potential was more realized by the Android phone [developed by Google and partners through the Open Handset Alliance]," Mura says. "The iPhone didn't connect with our consumers because it's a closed environment. It was expensive. You had to get it at AT&T. Our guys didn't like all those restrictions. The iPhone created the sense of urgency around the mobile industry. It really created the possibilities and I would argue, for our consumer, the Android delivered it.

"You could get an Android with any carrier. You can get it on numerous devices. You can go and shop and find the best phone that fits for you but the good news was if you were a guy 21 to 29, you have to have it and it's your best friend. It's the best thing that has ever happened to you. You would rather lose your wallet than lose your phone."

The first commercially available phone to run Android was the HTC Dream, released in late 2008. By late 2011, Android had eclipsed Apple's market share.

25

Belle Tire Rolls with Mobile

ONE OF THE MOST noteworthy programs in 2010 integrated mobile with traditional media. Belle Tire, 88 years old and the nation's eighth-largest tire retailer with 84 stores in Michigan and Ohio, added a mobile call to action to its television and radio buys and other marketing programs with the Detroit Red Wings, Detroit Pistons, and Michigan State Spartans.

Here's how it worked:

Belle Tire first offered a free set of tires in a text-to-win promotion where consumers texted-in the word *Tire* to Belle Tire's short code. All who entered received a $20-off mobile coupon. Participants were then invited to join the Belle Tire Advantage Club—and 55 percent opted in to the club. In a follow-up campaign, 77 percent of participants subsequently joined the mobile Advantage Club. Belle Tire and Hipcricket conducted multivariant analysis to determine which ad executions and channels were most effective and produced the best return on investment.

"By adding a mobile element, we were able to track which ads were the most successful, which helps us to better plan our budgets for future campaigns," says Don Barnes, marketing manager at Belle

Tire. "In addition, we've gained a database of customers who we're now able to communicate with on an ongoing basis—this hyperlocal mobile engagement is very valuable. We like to reward our loyal customers, and mobile has been a great venue to help us do it—more so than e-mail and other types of campaigns we've tried."

Key Takeaways

- The newest technology can succeed for even the oldest brands.
- Belle Tire wisely used its database to give back to its customers rather than to solely target prospects.
- The tire retailers used different keywords in different media, ensuring that it could measure each individually.

Also in 2010, the Hipcricket advertising and marketing network grew 10-fold due to demonstrable increases in brand awareness, customer acquisition, and in-store traffic. With approximately 50 percent coming from repeat customers, the network was used by companies in more than 15 industries, including quick service restaurants (QSR), retail, travel, technology, and consumer packaged goods (CPG).

According to Hipcricket figures, 55 percent of the ads were delivered via short message service (SMS) and 45 percent through display advertising on mobile websites and in mobile application banners.

Then in late 2010, Steve Mura and MillerCoors, the second-largest beer company in America, poured more into mobile.

"I inherited a technology platform that was rigid and it was not clear what it was intended to do," Mura, MillerCoors's director of digital marketing, says. "My job was to pull both these ropes together and to lay out a clear strategy of how are we going to use digital and connect with our consumers and sell more beer and what are the technologies and platforms we need to have in place to make that happen faster, smarter, and have us leaning forward and flexible.

"When I got here, I was looking at all these statements of work and we were paying lots of money per program to set up a text, get a short code, turn these programs on, get the copy, creative, and go."

Mura quickly figured that it was time to identify one trusted and accountable mobile partner.

"What was said was there's got to be a better way so we went out to talk to a bunch of people like the Hipcrickets of the world," he says. "We said, 'These are how many programs we are doing, this is how much we spend on it. Come back to us with a solution to how we can have economies of scale both in thinking and in actual dollars and technology.'

"Where most people struggle about the Hipcrickets of the world is if you don't have a clear strategy about how digital can help you with your business. It has to be specific to your business. What most people have is what I call a generic digital playbook. Meaning trying digital is important so 'We're going to use digital—we're going to use Foursquare and Facebook and Google and all these folks.'"

Mura calls that a recipe for disaster.

"What happens is every technology is fair game," he says. "What happens when you get a clear strategy is you say, 'Here are my goals in digital. This is what I need digital to do to help me sell more beer.' It becomes very obvious that when you meet partners like Hipcricket and you need technology that other folks can help you with—there are other people who built really cool businesses and have really good technology but they won't help you get to where you need to go.

"That's the fundamental place we are in as an industry—there are those who get digital and know how to use it to help their business and those who know digital is important and just go out there and flounder in the space for the next couple of years because they're going to say Facebook is just as fair game as Google search or as Foursquare. What they're going to find is half of those things weren't built intended to build their businesses. That's a costly and long lesson to learn."

Mura insisted that those at MillerCoors spending the mobile budget had a clear purpose in mind.

"My team did have some money that we knew we were going to allocate to mobile," he says. "The bigger transformation for us, at least internally, was to make sure all the field marketers, brand marketers, and retail customer marketers that we have in this building started to have a mobile first strategy.

"'Why is the mobile device so important to our guys? How do your plans and programs play a role on that mobile device? How should I be thinking about it? What devices are our guys on?' So really part of it for me was funding it and part of it was education—the importance of mobile and why we're doubling down. Why all the brands [within MillerCoors] should put more money there. We want everything in the company to be mobile-enabled."

Following an extensive review process, Mura and his team chose Hipcricket as its exclusive mobile marketing and mobile advertising partner. Hipcricket signed a three-year contract to develop and execute all mobile marketing efforts in conjunction with MillerCoors's agency and development partners.

Among the reasons for its decision, MillerCoors cited Hipcricket's mobile marketing and mobile advertising capabilities and experience, its technology platform, its bilingual client and creative services staff and expertise in marketing to Hispanics, and its creative and strategic services capabilities.

"Every job and company has a signature deal and MillerCoors was the signature deal for Hipcricket," says Doug Stovall, Hipcricket's senior vice president of sales and client services. "Because MillerCoors is such a phenomenal customer and will try so many things, it gave us an opportunity to do a lot of stuff. It allowed the Hipcricket people to believe in our potential."

Hipcricket chief operating officer Eric Harber agrees.

"I remember reading that RFP [request for proposal]," he says. "That was the most sophisticated RFP in mobile I'd seen from a brand to that date. Period. It was really indicative. We had to go through a security audit and all sorts of special hoops. At the time, it was painful but we ended up prevailing.

"One of the reasons why was we had prepared for that—we were a company that was thinking beyond next week, next month, six months from now. We were thinking, 'How do you service the needs of some of the most trusted brands in the world with the most rigorous design needs to accomplish their goals?' That's when we really shined. It was exciting. It kind of demonstrated what this 'more than SMS' [short message service] company strategy was about. It was the perfect picture of how that came together."

Hipcricket staff saw that side of the win as well.

"Our employees get excited when they get to push the envelope," Harber says. "They get to meet the needs of their customers in a pragmatic way but also do it with elegance. To do it with the pedestrian technology that absolutely works but also to be able to push the envelope just enough to be exciting and engaging but not so far that it's just flight of fancy and it's just for the sake of doing something wild and crazy and off the edge that doesn't produce results."

Mura's team learned from the early campaigns and saw the benefits.

"I think we're there as a company but it took about 12 to 18 months," he says. "It wasn't that people didn't put mobile in their programs [before]. They needed stories [case studies] to say, 'Okay, I did it and now I'm going to put dollars behind it into the platform and into mobile overall.'"

26

Other Brands Produce Notable Campaigns

Macy's: Mobile as the Ticket to Backstage

As Patrick Flanagan of Simon Malls explained earlier in the book, mobile provides a unique and mostly untapped avenue to engage shoppers at the point of sale.

There is more than a bit of irony in the fact that arguably the most innovative retailer when it comes to mobile is Hipcricket client Macy's, the venerable department store that first opened its doors in 1858.

For several years, Macy's has used mobile to make its advertising interactive and to grow its database.

In early 2011, Macy's developed a differentiating in-store program called Backstage Pass that gave shoppers access to 30-second videos that provided fashion tips and a behind-the-scenes look at clothes from Bobbi Brown, Sean "Diddy" Combs, Tommy Hilfiger, Michael Kors, Greg Norman for Tasso Elba, Rachel Roy, Irina Shabayeva for I.N.C., and Martha Stewart.

Later that year, the program went mainstream with a Macy's Backstage Pass television spot that showed how quick response (QR) codes work and offered customers the chance to win Macy's shopping sprees. Starring Combs, Hilfiger, Roy, Jessica Simpson, and Stewart, the 30-second spot aired nationwide.

Key Takeaways

- The program was truly multichannel with Macy's giving shoppers the choice of interacting via short message service (SMS), multimedia messaging (MMS), QR code, and the mobile Web.
- Star power brought more attention to the campaign and further educated the public on how to combine mobile with the shopping experience.
- Macy's learned from its first Backstage Pass effort, making its second more valuable to customers.

Perrier: Hot, Hot, Hot

Perrier, one of the most identifiable brands in the world, is often the sparkling water choice of the Boomer and older generations. To make it cooler to younger demographics, the Nestlé-owned manufacturer turned up the heat in its Le Club Perrier promotion with a multifaceted mobile program developed with Hipcricket.

Important elements included mobile websites created in English and French, QR codes, and interactive voice response (IVR) technology, but what made the campaign memorable was the optimized-for-mobile YouTube videos that got hotter or more provocative, the more they were viewed.

Consumers could join the Le Perrier Club party by scanning QR codes or texting *Party* to a short code. Perrier advertised the promotion at numerous retail locations where its beverages are sold.

Cocktail napkins with what looked like a handwritten phone number jotted on them encouraged consumers to call the number. When they did, a woman who seemed to be at a party picked up and told the caller to press 1 to get directions to the party. When the caller followed the direction, a message was sent to his or her mobile phone with a link to the mobile page.

"We wanted our Le Club campaign to tell a story—to be seamless, memorable, and viral. To do that, we needed social media, and we needed mobile," says Michele Vieira, Perrier brand manager. "The mobile interaction was critical and Hipcricket was able to help us develop the type of engaging experience consumers remembered and talked about."

Key Takeaways

- Sex sells to a younger demographic (you think?).
- It was critical that the video experience was first class to meet the brand's needs and expectations.
- Running the program in multiple languages ensured that more would be able to participate.

Ford Has a Better Idea

In the late 1960s automotive giant Ford advertised that it had "a better idea." In 2011, it was still delivering on the promise.

Breaking from the pack in the most active advertising category in the United States, FordDirect, a joint venture between Ford Motor Company and its dealers, announced a mobile service that enabled shoppers to receive prompt, targeted information about Ford vehicles by sending a text message. Powered by Hipcricket, the service used unique and innovative processes that integrate Ford brand print and television advertising to deliver information specific to the vehicles of interest to the customer.

For example, those watching a Ford Fusion television commercial could text *Fusion* to a short code to receive local offers. Viewers were then prompted to text their zip code and applicable incentives were sent. Consumers were then given the option to text their name if they would like to be contacted by their local dealer.

How was this a "better idea"?

Providing benefits to consumers and local dealers, the effort generated a 14 percent lead conversion rate.

"Our mobile service enables customers to engage with us immediately while their questions are top of mind," says Valerie Fuller, chief operating officer at FordDirect. "The service also delivers additional customer referrals to Ford dealerships, enabling them to quickly reach out to the customer regarding the specific vehicle they are interested in."

Key Takeaways

- The campaign proved that consumers would be open to being contacted by a car dealer if there was perceived value.
- Mobile provided immediacy, giving Ford the chance to capitalize on high-potential leads.
- Ford could personalize its follow-up, knowing through the mobile interaction which model most interested the consumer.

27

Trends

The Convergence of Mobile and Social

Facebook Mobilizes

We may be in what Kris Foley of Clear Channel refers to as a "time-crunched" society, but when it comes to sharing the minutiae in our lives, we always find a way.

Whether it's posting Halloween pictures of the kids or commenting on the new Chinese Chicken Salad at Applebee's, social networking is so prevalent that it is nothing short of a global phenomenon. And it is increasingly going mobile, understandable given the fact that social commentary can't wait until one gets home or, in many instances around the world, until the population adopts the personal computer. That day may never come.

By far, the most popular social network is Facebook, which as mentioned previously in this book, launched in 2004. As of July 2011, Facebook had more than 800 million members and publicly pointed to mobile as the way to continue growing.

The company says that it aims to have 500 million mobile users worldwide, a figure it knows it can reach only if it goes after all wireless subscribers—including the obvious owners of smartphones but also those in the United States and around the world who carry feature phones.

In the first half of 2011, the company launched a new mobile application, or app, to bring Facebook to the most popular and mainstream mobile phones around the world. According to Facebook, the app works on more than 2,500 devices from Nokia, Sony Ericsson, LG, and other manufacturers.

Although it may be focused on low-end phones, the experience is hardly low-end. In fact, the company cleverly positioned the app as a "better Facebook experience for our most popular features, including an easier-to-navigate home screen, contact synchronization, and fast scrolling of photos and friend updates."

Facebook worked with mobile operators worldwide to make mobile users an enticing offer: a chance to try the app for 90 days without paying for data charges. More than a dozen mobile operators signed on, including Dialog (Sri Lanka), Life (Ukraine), Play (Poland), StarHub (Singapore), STC (Saudi Arabia), Three (Hong Kong), Tunisiana (Tunisia), Viva (Dominican Republic), and Vodafone (Romania).

Facebook's mission statement is to "help you connect and share with the people in your life." Of note, it doesn't say, "help you connect on a personal computer."

Hipcricket did its part in bringing social and mobile together. By early 2011, the company had introduced SocialConnect, a platform feature that gave consumers the ability to join a brand's mobile loyalty club simply by clicking on a link off the brand's Facebook page. Through SocialConnect, advertisers could capture multiple levels of opt-in data from their Facebook fans, including e-mail addresses, mobile phone numbers, and locations. SocialConnect also integrated seamlessly into a company's existing mobile and e-mail databases and reduced the cost of acquiring customer data while leveraging the power of the Facebook platform.

Twitter Takes Off

Not nearly as ubiquitous, Twitter has nonetheless become a forum for members to share the details of their lives, often via mobile. Although news personality Katie Couric has said that "no one gives a rat's ass" what she had for lunch, the fact is that many people indeed do. To prove that point, all one needs to do is look at the celebrity Kardashian family, masters of combining reality television with Twitter to drive its brand. Near the end of 2011, Kim Kardashian had eclipsed 11 million Twitter followers.

For those who have lived on another planet the last few years, Twitter is a social networking and microblogging service that enables its users to send and read posts of up to 140 characters. By 2011, five years after it launched, there were 200 million members, opening up a new avenue for brands to reach their customers and prospects.

Feature Phones; Smartphones; They Are All Megaphones

Indicators including age and years ingrained in traditional media would make Hank Wasiak an unlikely candidate to push new media change. But those indicators don't take into account Wasiak's decades-long quest to reach consumers in more personal ways.

For the 68-year-old Wasiak, social and mobile have changed everything.

"I always had a hunger for what was next," says Wasiak, the once youngest-ever vice president at famed ad agency Doyle Dane Bernbach who went on to become vice chairman of McCann Erickson WorldGroup before cofounding The Concept Farm. "At a time in my career when I probably should've been winding it down, along came all this shift and it reenergized me. Six, seven, eight years ago, you couldn't get people to talk about this because there was very much a closed mentality.

"How has it changed from the pre-Internet age to mobile and now? It was all about the 'broadcast out' impressions to the creation of expressions that involves the community of people. It's more the age of conversation than the art of broadcast."

Wasiak defines the roles of the marketer and consumer this way:

"The consumer is in control. All of these things are just so real and apparent. There's one key thing that a lot of people miss when we talk about the consumer being in control, and there is no question that they are. They're in control of the marketing messages that go out. What I hope never changes, and some of it scares me a little bit because I hear brand people say that we have to give up control of our brand to the consumer. My pushback on that is no frickin' way.

Controlling your brand now is more important than ever and you have to exercise exceptionally tight control.

"I just have a pretty simple checklist—it's a rock-solid brand position that is formed by consumer insights. So you're constantly now listening and looking. Once you have that position, you must not consider it a nice to have. You must infuse it emotionally and rationally into every aspect of your company and business. When you communicate it, it's got to be communicated very respectfully and in a way that's on the consumer's terms and then you have to deliver it constantly. Once you're confident in that, that's when you let the product or brand go and let the consumer have a great time with it. Then follow through with it."

Wasiak's indoctrination into social came during a conference hosted by Jeff Pulver, an Internet pioneer and early investor in Twitter.

"I met a couple of people who were saying some very smart things," Wasiak says. "There was nobody else from the agency business there. I said let me find out what these people were all about. They were renegades. They were different.

"In the early days of the social community, the thing that struck me the most—I came out of a business—the advertising business—that was very difficult, very competitive. You didn't give a competitor an edge. You didn't share a thing and if anybody came near your client, you put up the wall and the moat. In the social world that was emerging in a great way, it was just the opposite. Everybody wanted to share. It was very democratic. They were giving away the secret, their point of view, and I found that extremely refreshing. I thought that was terrific."

Moments of Trust

In 2002, I began to examine the importance of what I call *Moments of Trust*, consumer touch points with brands that influence trial, sales, and loyalty. A decade ago, the poor customer service delivered by retailers and others had begun reaching such extremes that it began to send people away angry and vowing never to return.

By 2010, global consulting firm Accenture had reported that 64 percent of consumers had switched companies in the past year due to poor customer service. Further, the company reported that 54 percent of global consumers were not willing to compromise on levels of customer service, product options, product quality, and frequency of communications with companies in exchange for lower prices.

Coinciding with that report, by the start of the century's second decade, mobile had clearly shifted the dynamic in retail aisles. One could easily see how shoppers were using their cell phones to check prices and read reviews, and when they experienced something they liked or hated, they used their devices like megaphones to tell the world about it.

To gauge the impact on brands and *Moments of Trust*, in early 2011, I commissioned a representative survey of U.S. feature phone and smartphone owners.

Here's what I found:

- 46 percent reported they communicated with friends, family, and their social network following a positive in-store experience.
- 40 percent said they used their phone in a retail location to detail a negative interaction.
- Of those who used their devices to communicate brand experiences, 18 percent used Facebook; 8 percent employed Twitter; and 32 percent communicated via text message.
- 10 percent said they had heard from a brand following a post on a social network about a retail interaction.
- 35 percent said they would want to hear from a store or brand after a negative experience.
- 34 percent said they had seen a post from someone in their network.
- 48 percent said they would be influenced by a post.

What did this *Moments of Trust* survey really tell us?

In my view, nothing had changed and everything had changed. Since day one of commerce, it has been critical to serve the customer. That is, of course, still true today. What is dramatically different is the consumer's ability to broadcast his or her experiences and to influence consideration and purchase patterns.

Responding at the Point of Impression

Nearly 15 years ago, brand marketer and author Rick Mathieson began tying together mobile and new business practices. Though he was ahead of his time, Mathieson's vision became reality years later.

"I started asking the question: What does mobile mean to businesses trying to keep up with—and serve—the increasingly mobile masses?" he says. "What happens when eyeballs we once aggregated by gross ratings points and mass markets now gather in social networks or even micromarkets of one? How do we redefine advertising and the brand experience when the most direct link to consumers is less and less the 52-inch flat screen TV in the living room, or the 17-inch laptop PC [personal computer], and more and more the completely personal, interactive device in the hands of virtually every man, woman, and child?"

Now, Mathieson, author of *The On-Demand Brand* and *Branding Unbound*, counsels brands to turn what were passive activities into interactive ones.

"If it makes sense for their marketing and communications objectives, I advise them to integrate mobile into the media mix by making it a response mechanism to their print, their direct mail, their outdoor, their TV, their radio, and other advertising channels," he says. "Never again should a target consumer scratch their head and say to themselves, 'What was that website I was going to look up, or that product I wanted to buy?' Now consumers can respond to commercial messages right at the point of impression.

"And that interaction should be of value to the consumer and bring the consumer a step closer in the buying process. Depending on how a promotion is set up, it might mean coupons sent to your mobile phone; you might access a mobile promo site; you might dial up a call center; you might watch a video demonstration; you might access shopper reviews; or you might even place a transaction, right at the point of impression. It's about determining if mobile makes sense given the marketer's objectives, how it can best be utilized to help meet those objectives."

2011 as Year of Mobile Commerce

Elsewhere in this book, I write that the mere mention of the phrase *The Year of Mobile* gives me a queasy stomach. There just is no clear-cut, agreed upon time when mobile met a tipping point.

But when it comes to *The Year of Mobile Commerce*, there is much less dispute. How do I know that it was 2011? Consumers showed us by their actions, reaching for their mobile phones at every step of the consumer journey, from researching products to making purchases.

Before the season began, InsightExpress's third-quarter 2011 Digital Consumer Portrait found that 32 percent of consumers planned to use their mobile devices to help research products by comparison shopping, and 27 percent said they would use their mobile devices to read reviews while in the store.

How did it play out?

IBM's Smarter Commerce initiative produced an online retail benchmark study, research that compared Cyber Monday (the Monday after Thanksgiving) 2011 to Cyber Monday 2010 and reveals some surprising trends. The early 2011 holiday season findings were based on data from IBM Coremetrics Benchmark, an analytics-based, peer-level benchmarking solution that measures online marketing results, including real-time sales data from the websites of more than 500 U.S. retailers. All of the data were aggregated and anonymous.

Predictably, consumers were willing to spend more when shopping on the Internet. Online sales in the United States were up 33 percent over 2010, with consumers pushing the average order value up from $193.24 to $198.26 (an increase of 2.6 percent). The real news was our increasing reliance on mobile. Specifically, 10.8 percent of Internet shoppers used a mobile device to visit a retailer's site, up from 3.9 percent in 2010. Additionally, mobile sales grew dramatically, reaching 6.6 percent on Cyber Monday versus 2.3 percent in 2010.

How did Cyber Monday 2011 compare to Black Friday 2011?

- Online sales were up 29.3 percent over Black Friday.
- On Cyber Monday mobile traffic averaged 10.8 percent, compared with 14.3 percent on Black Friday.
- Consumer sales on mobile devices reached 6.6 percent on Cyber Monday versus 9.8 percent on Black Friday.
- Apple's iPhone and iPad continued to rank one and two for mobile device retail traffic (4.1 percent and 3.3 percent, respectively). Android maintained its position in third at 3.2 percent. Collectively iPhone and iPad accounted for 7.4 percent of all online retail traffic on Cyber Monday versus 10.2 percent on Black Friday.
- Shoppers using the iPad also continued to drive more retail purchases than any other device, with conversion rates reaching 5.2 percent on Cyber Monday compared with 4.6 percent on Black Friday.

How did the holiday shopping season fare worldwide? According to PayPal, Black Friday global mobile payment volume increased six-fold (516 percent) compared with 2010. The company released the following data:

- Between 1 and 2 PM Pacific Standard Time (PST) was the busiest mobile shopping hour on Black Friday 2011.
- Black Friday global mobile payment volume more than doubled (148 percent) compared with an average Friday.
- PayPal saw a 371 percent increase in the number of customers shopping through mobile on Black Friday 2011 compared with 2010.
- Shoppers in these cities made the most mobile purchases through PayPal on Black Friday: New York, Houston, Miami (Florida), Los Angeles, and Chicago.

How about PayPal's Cyber Monday 2011 shopping data?

- PayPal Mobile announced a 552 percent increase in global mobile payment volume on Cyber Monday 2011 compared with Cyber Monday 2010.
- There was a 397 percent increase in the number of customers shopping through PayPal Mobile on Cyber Monday 2011 compared with 2010.
- On Cyber Monday 2011, PayPal saw global mobile payment volume up 154 percent compared with an average Monday.
- Cyber Monday 2011 resulted in a 17 percent increase in global mobile payment volume compared with Black Friday 2011.
- On Cyber Monday 2011, consumers shopped on mobile most frequently between 2 and 3 PM PST.
- Shoppers in these cities made the most mobile purchases through PayPal on Cyber Monday 2011: New York, Chicago, Los Angeles, Houston, and Miami.

During the holiday period, comScore released a study on U.S. mobile retail usage based on data from its comScore Mobile Retail Advisor report. The results showed that 38 percent of smartphone owners had used their phone to make a purchase at least once in the course of their device ownership.

Digital content purchases, such as music, e-books, TV episodes, and movies, were the most popular mobile purchases in September 2011 with 47 percent of smartphone purchasers buying these items. Thirty-seven percent purchased clothing or accessories directly from a retailer, and 35 percent of purchasers bought event tickets. Slightly more than one in three mobile purchasers bought daily deals and gift certificates on their device during the month.

Analysis of where consumers were located when they purchased products/services on their smartphone found that 56 percent did so while at home, leading as the most popular purchase location. Forty-two percent of consumers made purchases while out of the home (e.g., restaurants, parks, etc.) or at work, with 37 percent making purchases while traveling/commuting. Slightly more than one in three purchasers used their smartphone to make a purchase while in a store, highlighting the increasingly important role mobile is playing in consumers' brick-and-mortar retail experience, especially as a tool for real-time price and product comparisons.

Slightly less than half of all mobile phone consumers engaged in shopping activities on their mobile device. comScore said that the marketer's focus should be on the smartphone platform because two-thirds of this audience use their device for shopping activities.

Even for smartphone owners who have highly capable devices, taking a picture of a product was the most popular shopping activity at 37 percent, followed by searching for a nearby store at 32 percent. Two-fifths of the smartphone audience has made a purchase using their mobile phone.

Privacy Concerns or Win-Win Customer Relationship Management?

The naysayers suggest that the mobile phone provides the ultimate tracking tool to know a user's location and just about everything else about him or her. Where does the mobile subscriber browse? Which products does he or she buy? How much time is spent in the tanning salon? Or worse.

The issue of privacy is not unique to mobile. The watchdogs have long accused entities as large as Facebook, Google, and Apple of deceptive practices on the Web. As recently as late 2011, a front-page *USA Today* headline read, "How Facebook Tracks You Across the Web."

Privacy questions go back much further than that.

In late 2011, Facebook agreed to settle Federal Trade Commission (FTC) charges that it deceived consumers by telling them they could keep their information on Facebook private, and then repeatedly allowing it to be shared and made public. The proposed settlement required Facebook to take several steps to make sure it lives up to its promises in the future, including giving consumers clear and prominent notice and obtaining consumers' express consent before their information is shared beyond the privacy settings they have established.

According to the FTC:

- In December 2009, Facebook changed its website so certain information that users may have designated as private—such as their Friends List—was made public. They didn't warn users that this change was coming, or get their approval in advance.
- Facebook represented that third-party applications (apps) that users installed would have access only to user information that they needed to operate. In fact, the apps could access nearly all of users' personal data—data the apps didn't need.
- Facebook told users they could restrict sharing of data to limited audiences—for example, with Friends Only. In fact, selecting Friends Only did not prevent their information from being shared with third-party applications their friends used.
- Facebook had a Verified Apps program and claimed it certified the security of participating apps. It didn't.
- Facebook promised users that it would not share their personal information with advertisers. It did.
- Facebook claimed that when users deactivated or deleted their accounts, their photos and videos would be inaccessible. But Facebook allowed access to the content, even after users had deactivated or deleted their accounts.

As for the prevalence of spam, the mobile industry has made concerted efforts to not repeat mistakes made on the Internet.

In late 2011, the Mobile Marketing Association (MMA) Privacy and Advocacy Committee, made up of representatives from all parts of the mobile ecosystem, released a mobile application policy framework it says should be used as a starting point for most mobile applications. It stated that the core goal was to encourage the mobile application developer community to continue to move consumer privacy interests forward.

Included was direction on communicating to end users what information the application obtains, how it will be used, and language to permit the mobile subscriber to opt out. It specifically gave guidance to those developing applications to be used by children and those that include medical data that is protected by federal and other laws.

The policy is a companion to the MMA's Global Code of Conduct document and the extensive direction put out by the MMA's Consumer Best Practices Committee governing the rules and regulations with regard to messaging.

Such entities as Microsoft are advocating for transparency. In 2011, Microsoft identified what it said was unintended behavior in the Windows Phone software involving location services, namely the tracking of users off of certain camera-related features and through voice commands such as "Find Pizza."

It took quick steps to explain how it was eliminating that behavior through a software update, and reminded device owners that they could prevent access to location information if they chose to do so.

Hipcricket has also proactively addressed privacy issues, using its patented technology to work with clients to provide personalized marketing messages that do not cross over to invasion.

"There's a trade-off between privacy and customization and we never want to walk that line," says Hipcricket chief technology officer Nathaniel Bradley. "We have technologies that allow for the consumer to opt in and to engage with the brands on a long-term basis to create the ongoing dialogue and interactive communication that mobile enables. In an opt-in situation, everyone is happy. In the situation where you want to target an advertisement to an end user and utilize information that characterizes the end user, we do so in a fashion that protects privacy, that honors privacy and that utilizes anonymous data collection capability.

"We have a patent pending that we call the 'ant farm' invention. We don't care about a particular ant or consumer in the marketplace; we simply care about the consumer's behavior in aggregate. The brand doesn't necessarily want to know your identity, your phone number, and social security number. They want to know your behavior within their ecosphere, within their retail outlet. You want to ensure that you engage with a mobile marketing entity that has both a policy toward consumer privacy and a proactive approach to protect consumer privacy. There is a natural negative to targeting which is an intrusion of privacy—any type of Big Brother approach is not good for a brand to invoke upon a consumer."

Y&R's Thom Kennon, a longtime international marketer, believes that consumers willingly give their information to brands when they see value in doing so.

"I have some controversial views but I believe privacy is delusional," he says. "I don't think for the last 70 or 80 years of consumerism have we enjoyed this Pollyannaish view of what privacy and data protection we were going to have. I don't believe even aspirationally that it's attainable. I believe smart brands, smart platforms, smart publishers have figured out ways to create a value equation with consumers that says if you surrender a number of data points, you're going to get better stuff. You're going to get less clutter, less advertising, and going to get more personalized, more tailored content and service, and there's a huge benefit to both of us to do that.

"For 50 or 60 years, some of us have sat around traditional terrestrial television and watched for every 30 minutes of content, about 5 or 6 minutes of advertising. That was a contract we had with the brands and the networks to subsidize the cost of all that wonderful content."

Kennon sees a similar contract happening via wireless devices.

"The mobile touch point will be the most essential, primary thumbprint for ongoing CRM [customer relationship management] programs," he says. "Whether you're in financial services, whether you're in consumer product goods, whether you're in personal technology, whether you're in retail, every brand I believe has enough skin in the game to protect the investment in acquiring customers by retaining them.

"I think CRM will be baked in an investable price of a brand's marketing and advertising budgets which right now they are not for many brands. They're just constantly reacquiring the same customers. CRM becomes the next big thing in mobile. You incentivize people with points, you incentivize them with the social currency of being proud owners of your brand. Without a doubt it will be the place where the smartest brands in each category are going to move very quickly."

28

Innovation

Emergence of Multiscreen Marketing

The Introduction of Tablets

For a company that oozes innovation, Apple was behaving fairly generically when it came to its marketing messaging surrounding the introduction of the iPad in January 2010.

"Magical & Revolutionary Device at an Unbelievable Price" read the subhead on the press release.

Given that it was distributed during the month of the enormous and noisy International Consumer Electronics Show in Las Vegas, Nevada, there were surely thousands of press releases that were making a similar claim.

But Apple may have been the only one that delivered.

Years after Apple chief executive officer (CEO) Steve Jobs dismissed the idea of bringing a tablet to market, Apple launched the device with what it called a "responsive high-resolution Multi-Touch™ display" that allowed users to physically interact with applications and content.

The iPad was just 0.5-inch thick and weighed just 1.5 pounds—thinner and lighter than any laptop or netbook.

Connectivity was made possible through Wi-Fi or via a mobile operator's network. Every application, with the total nearly 140,000, worked in portrait and landscape, reacting to the movement of the user.

The price was $499.

"iPad creates and defines an entirely new category of devices that will connect users with their apps [applications] and content in a much more intimate, intuitive, and fun way than ever before," Jobs said.

What quickly became clear was that young, old, and everywhere in between would appreciate the features and benefits. In restaurants and on planes, it quickly became common to see toddlers and their older siblings playing games and using the iPad as a tool for learning. Conversely, Boomers and older generations took to the device, in large part because the user experience was so intuitive and the size of words and images could be enlarged just by touching the screen.

"The Boomer market, if you look at [age] 41 plus, has 91 percent of the net assets and people are not thinking about the affluent or the older woman as a consumer at all," says Mary Furlong, among the world's experts on marketing to the Boomer and older demographics. "She is totally written off yet they're very technology-savvy in part because of the influence their children and grandchildren have had on the way they communicate. Nothing matters more to them than family, and the way the family communicates is through text. They're going to become early adopters of that technology whether it's Skype [a VOIP, or voice-over Internet protocol] or FaceTime [Apple's video conference application] or Facebook.

"The iPad is the ultimate Boomer product in terms of visibility and change of font size but no one would describe it as a Boomer product. Many Boomers suffer from insomnia so whether it's listening to the radio at night or listening to audiobooks or having something there when you travel that you can connect home with, the iPad is the product."

Reaching Beyond Boomers

"The most important thing to get to an 80-year-old who is going into assisted living is mobile technology—that is their lifeline and probably the entertainment is the iPad after having a spouse for 50 years to talk to and then not having that there," says Furlong.

"Health concerns and convenience are other drivers toward mobile adoption. With diabetes such a big problem, there are a whole slew of products that can remind you with couponing and messaging about your weight. That industry can send you a message reminding you to walk the dog each day or to eat healthy. No one has been very creative. If you're less mobile, you're going to say, 'I don't want to go to Macy's to do my shopping. I want to be able to purchase online and on mobile.'"

Better Life, Better Sex, Meet New People

AARP, the world's largest nonprofit organization helping people 50 years old and older improve their lives, holds similar views when it comes to the difference tablets and mobile phones are making.

"I think there's definitely the perception that Boomers, especially older Boomers, are not as tech savvy as other generations," says Nataki Edwards, the organization's vice president of marketing, digital strategy, and operations. "To some degree their behavior and consumption is different but there has been irrefutable data that shows adoption and the Boomers with the iPad, just to name one point, that should have put some of those perceptions to bed.

"I think it's the personality of Boomers. They are a generation that really wants to be on the cutting edge. They don't want to feel like they're left behind or old—and they are not. Some of this is, 'I'm going to know what's going on and not be left behind as this technology train is moving.' It's become less of connecting with friends and family—that's the easy answer. It's much more personal for them. How can they get more information and have a better life, have better sex, meet new people? All of these things play into technology and how much they use it. They want to make their lives faster, easier, and better as well."

Tablets to Rule the World?

Kennon from Y&R sees tablets as much more than a stop along the technology road.

"It's a step change," Kennon says. "It's not even an extension of the smartphone. Future mobile computing is based a lot on what the tablets look like today."

While Kennon credits Apple for its iPad innovation, he sees Amazon as further moving the ball.

"The Kindle Fire has brought down the price point," he says of Amazon's tablet offering that was introduced in the fall of 2011 for $199. "We're seeing this massive reshift, almost a shakeup in expectations of what these devices must do, are able to do, and all in a range of use cases for a range of consumers.

"You make a mistake if you think this is a device. It's a service function thing. Amazon is in the services business. This becomes the stickiest thing since a toothbrush on the road for about everybody in the world. This is a portable device that gets me to all of my stuff—my services, my content, my documents, my music, my art, my whatever. Tablets are completely breaking open marketing, communications, publishing, advertising, and education."

To make his point about the significance of tablets, Kennon, who has worked all around the world, points to the introduction of government-subsidized $35 tablets put into the hands of citizens of India.

"These things will be like bicycles in certain cities in Europe," Kennon says. "In the '30s and '40s, [bicycles] were on every doorstep and people had an honor system for borrowing and using them. I believe tablets will become completely ubiquitous.

"Tablets require an entirely different strategy than a mobile phone. Tablets require an entirely different strategy from the fixed Web. We don't know enough about what we don't know of the sort of change this will drive but it's going to democratize access to the mobile Web and change the face, I think, of how brands get customers through interactive channels forever."

We are already seeing some of that happening at CNN, which began as a cable news operation in 1980 and now extends to nine cable and satellite television networks; one private place-based network; two radio networks; wireless devices around the world; CNN Digital Network, a network of news websites in the United States; CNN Newsource, a global syndicated news service; and strategic international partnerships within both television and the digital media.

CNN Reaches the World's Audiences in New Ways

"This is about engaging consumers across CNN platforms and at the end of it, affecting and enhancing the way consumers see the CNN brand," says Louis Gump, CNN vice president of mobile. "That's also true of our distributors and advertisers.

"I only have a few overall guidelines for how we build the business. One of them is for each platform, start first with the assumption that that platform is different from the others and work backward to the similarities instead of the other way around. Sometimes it's tempting to say a mobile phone looks like a PC [personal computer], it's just smaller. That turns out not to be the case for lots of reasons, including these days touchscreens, location, the personal association with the device, etc. We fundamentally believe that there are at least four or five device platforms and these are TV, PC, tablet, and phone and you can make an argument for lots of others ranging from game consoles to refrigerators. Each one of these ought to be treated differently."

Gump sees the mobile phone as the most ubiquitous and personal.

"In particular in the case of phones, you often see people who have these devices with them all the time," he says. "A bunch of us are more likely to say we'll leave our wallet at home than leave our phone. It's a device that's very present and very personal.

"On the other hand, if you look at tablets, which have kind of emerged in the last couple of years, what you see typically is a more immersive experience. People on average are going to be looking at it longer. They're going to dig down. There's less snacking [viewing small pieces of content] although there is plenty of that. And there's more, 'I just want to kick back and learn about something.' We see both of these, especially because it tends to be a touchscreen experience."

Gump further views the mix this way:

"If you look at the PC today, it tends to be a larger screen. It tends to be fixed—although many people use laptops—it tends not to be touchscreen, and it tends not to be location dependent. And TVs have their different experiences, too. There are different ways to look at each one and what's emerging now is the idea of dual screen usage. If you have a person sitting on a sofa with a tablet or a phone and they're watching a TV, there are some interesting things you can do to reach them and editorially we can tailor our content to them as well.

"Here's my premise—I believe that mobile is as different as online as TV is for radio. We have only just begun to explore how these differences apply. If you look at our offerings today, on the one hand, you can do lots of stuff that works well on all of our platforms. For starters, we want a significant amount of consistency across our products. Our TV Everywhere product is a good example. Now we have an experience on four screens that is entirely consistent. On the other hand, if you look at our iPad app, it's very different from our PC site or our phone apps or the mobile Web. That's because we felt the experience on that should be different. For people, there is a real immersion and it knocks people's socks off. We feature different content. We organize it differently."

ESPN: Mobile Hits and Misses

Longtime sports anchor Chris Berman tells the story of the early days of ESPN when the sports cable network was misidentified as having something to do with the Spanish language (*español*).

When it comes to ESPN's first large efforts into mobile, one might say ESPN stood for especially novel but not especially successful.

Yes, ESPN offered marketers a meaningful advertising option way back in 2005, when it teamed with Yahoo! Search Marketing for contextual pay-per-click ads on ESPN's mobile website. Michael Bayle, who sold those ads to ESPN while at Yahoo!, says the auction's floor was 10 cents but moved close to a half-dollar as brands competed to be in one of the top three sponsored positions.

"When we looked at the KPIs [key performance indicators]," says Bayle, "the user experience was preserved because we put these links into places that were relevant around games and scores that the fans were seeking. From an economic standpoint, the KPIs were brilliant because you had marketers who were seeking access to these fans to pedal their wares inclusive of tickets, merchandise, posters, and meet and greets. Because of the brilliance of the auction model, there was no pricing that ESPN was required to set. Instead the market found value in what they were seeing in terms of return on investment by the fans interacting with those links. The results were such that from the outset of the program to conclusion, the revenue had increased between 300 and 400 percent.

"These were the first mobile ads in the United States, maybe the world, appearing on an auction basis, distributed in contextually relevant places on ESPN's mobile site. This predated AdMob [an advertising network founded in 2006 and later bought by Google for $750 million] and the other [mobile] ad networks."

Where the sports network saw failure was in its 2005 launch of an ESPN-branded phone operated as an MVNO (mobile virtual network operator) and run through a partnership with Sprint. Approximately 18 months before the iPhone revolutionized mobile, ESPN offered an application that could produce real-time scores, something fans then and now demand. The network eventually streamed the first live sporting event ever sent to a mobile device in the United States, a September 2006 football game between Michigan and Vanderbilt.

ESPN learned that fans weren't willing to get this information at any price. There was only one phone available at launch that sold for just under $400 and the cost for minutes and data usage was considerably higher than what consumers saw on other devices. Despite efforts to rebrand, introduce more phones, and push the price down, the effort was halted by the end of 2006, with the *Wall Street Journal* reporting that Mobile ESPN had fewer than 10,000 subscribers.

"With the ESPN phone, I think we had a lot of the right ideas but we were certainly ahead of our time," says John Kosner, senior vice president and general manager of ESPN Digital Media. "Rather than focus on the software angle where we specialize, we also found ourselves in the hardware business which is not our expertise. But we gained a lot of insights and many of the people who worked on the project are still with us and hugely influential in our current direction."

Then came 2007 and Apple's introduction of a revolutionary smartphone.

The iPhone Influence

There may be no brand that capitalized more on the arrival of the iPhone than ESPN. The network built robust applications to extend the company's reach beyond television and ESPN.com. It offered personalized content and access to content that was packaged in high resolution.

But much as MillerCoors experienced, mobile took off for ESPN in 2009, when Android entered the scene, offering consumers lower-priced smartphones and device and carrier choice.

Meanwhile, ESPN's strategy has always centered on inclusion. Early on, it gave consumers the ability to receive scores and sports information via alerts sent to any feature phone or smartphone that was SMS-enabled. In fact, by the end of 2011 ESPN said it was delivering an astounding 1 billion texts a month.

According to the network, approximately 120,000 were tapping into ESPN mobile in any given minute, up 45 percent over the previous year. Additionally, visits to ESPN properties were led by ESPN's flagship television channel, then ESPN2, followed by ESPN.com and ESPN mobile. If ESPN.com and ESPN mobile were totaled together, the network said, they would eclipse numbers from ESPN2.

"You have a variety of things going on," says Kosner, who leads all of ESPN's digital media properties, including ESPN.com, a worldwide online sports service; ESPN360.com, the live sports event broadband network from ESPN; and all content development for mobile, interactive television, interactive gaming, and other emerging digital media. "One is that the sophistication level of the devices improves dramatically every year to the point that you're carrying a very powerful small computer in your pocket. The combination of the personal nature of the device, the ability to get real-time information any time, and also separately the simultaneous explosion of social media, has created a tremendous environment for innovation on these devices, really led in part by sports because it just fits so naturally into what fans want, when they want it, and our ability to deliver that.

"Our research shows that there's about a one-third incremental audience that is only coming to us on mobile. We're able to reach more audiences. Obviously we want to reach everybody who is a big fan. While being on mobile does enable us to expand our audience, we're trying to do that in general with all the TV networks, all the radio, Spanish language, and any number of things."

By far, ESPN's most important wireless product is delivered via the mobile Web. According to the network, as of fall 2011, 20 million of the 100 million mobile Web users were coming to ESPN. Further, ESPN had a dominant category share, larger than the second-, third-, and fourth-place companies combined.

ESPN's Lineup of Products

Catering to a seemingly insatiable fan appetite, ESPN's mobile product lineup includes everything from the live streaming of programming 24 hours a day, seven days a week, to alerts, apps, and mobile Web properties.

Among those to keep an eye on is the WatchESPN app that sends live content to computers, mobile phones, and tablets. Programming from the product, which was released in April 2011, includes the NBA regular season and playoffs, the major golf championship tournaments, all four Grand Slam tennis events, and original shows such as *SportsCenter* and *Pardon the Interruption*, among others.

Live streams of all the WatchESPN programs are available at no additional cost to those who receive ESPN as part of their TV subscription from select cable providers. In addition, access to live programming on the ESPN3 channel of WatchESPN.com is available at no additional cost to those with subscriptions to participating high-speed Internet service providers.

As we will discuss later in this book, live mobile video has struggled in America due to such factors as the nation's reliance on cars rather than mass transit and the costs of mega data usage imposed by the carriers. ESPN says it is different because sports fans go to the best available screen to view games, and often have a television and tablet or smartphone running ESPN programming simultaneously.

ESPN's ScoreCenter app on the iPhone is available in English, Spanish, French, Italian, German, and Portuguese.

Also, ESPN Mobile TV sends 800 live sporting events to subscribers of Sprint and AT&T among other carriers. ESPN Video on Demand is available on Verizon as is Gamecast, which features video highlights and ESPN radio clips.

"It's a reach strategy," Kosner said. "One of the lessons that we learned on the Web was to not just serve the emerging broadband customer in the previous decade, but also the dial-up to AOL and Yahoo! customer and everyone else. Today we have about a 33 percent share of sports websites. On mobile, we have about two-thirds to 70 percent share because we learned the lesson to try to come up with products that serve everybody.

"That also gets to the global nature of the opportunity here. We would like to be able to serve any fan who has any kind of feature phone with any sort of level of Internet connectivity anywhere in the world beginning with at least a score in certain territories and being able to do the kind of advanced content that we have in the United States."

Michael Bayle, now senior vice president and general manager of mobile at ESPN, also stresses the need for access for all.

"Without question, our modus operandi is to reach fans wherever they may be," he says. "To keep mobile defined as something you can hold in your hands, inclusive of tablets, a strategy we've put forth is to ensure that our content one is renderable, so it's accessible on any of those devices, but furthermore that we can cater it and tailor it to some of the form functions that the devices allow—obviously having a touch site is part of that strategy.

"Think of what a fan is—fanatical and someone who will desperately seek out, at the expense of other items they may be focusing on like driving at times, to be abreast of the game and be in the know about either the individuals they are following or sports that they are following. Obviously ESPN carries a leadership position because of its pedigree in television and recently in digital and magazines."

The Fan Has a Voice

ESPN says that it receives daily comments from consumers that are read to help drive product and content direction.

"The fan feedback is very instructive as to usability, as to prioritization of stories, as to what features are added and when," Kosner says. "Frankly we're trying to take that fan approach and apply it to everything we do. It has been a hallmark of mobile but it should be part of any plan we do for any product."

Of course, part of the plan is to deliver experiences on all devices in a pleasing way.

"In terms of the video, I'd say most of it is repurposed short-form video content that has been produced on one of the TV networks," Kosner says. "We do original digital shows and clips and those are very popular. Separately from that, we create a ton of content on the website and in the magazine that is utilized on mobile. Most of the original content on mobile is alerts and other specialized content around live events. Increasingly it's one group creating that and putting it on any screen.

"We don't view this as we have a website and we have mobile. We have great content for fans that is made available for whatever screen they want. We prioritize screens and think of the context in which you use them and the size of the screens. The development of smart television sets means that you can create an end-to-end application, say ScoreCenter that you can get on your phone, you can get on your desktop, you can get on your big screen. There are different things possible with that based on the real estate you have but it's fundamentally the same content."

Serving All

Kosner and Bayle are device and operating system agnostic, but they do need to prioritize given the many thousands of devices available to consumers.

"I think that there are at least four operating systems that matter," Kosner says. "iOS [Apple's operating system], Android [running Google software], BlackBerry RIM, and Windows Mobile. I'm not including Symbian because it appears that Nokia is placing its bet with Windows Mobile. You have to be strong on all these platforms. Obviously Android is now the biggest. It's also the most challenging because it's where the [fewest] rules apply and the most iterations of it. iOS is a more organized closed system and has been there since the start. I don't feel that one is necessarily more important than the others. You have to do a really good job on all of them. Certainly at least at the moment, iOS and Android are taking up most of our time."

According to the network, in 2009, when Droid was introduced, Android had a 5 percent share of mobile Web traffic to ESPN. By late 2011 it was nearly 35 percent.

The End of the DVR?

One of the most impactful personal technology innovations recently was the introduction of so-called time shifting and the digital video recorder around the turn of the century. Quickly we seemingly all were TiVo'ing our favorite shows and watching them on our schedules.

But that was before real-time, all-the-time connectivity took hold and the masses began living on social networks like Facebook and Twitter where information was shared, not delayed.

Kosner and Bayle believe that the fan isn't about to time-shift the experience when he or she can share it with others.

"Sports are all about live," Kosner says. "You have to watch and experience the game live. You want to talk about it while it's happening. You want more information about the game or other games taking place at the same time. That's all central. The development of these social networks and utilities like Twitter take it up a level because it makes it apparent that much more is possible. Location-based content, the sharing of photos, the ability to watch video, and more."

Bayle says that the convergence of mobile and social changed the time-shifting model almost as fast as it appeared.

"I would argue that's the biggest interruption that has happened is because of the success of mobile," he says. "One to three years ago, one could comfortably record their favorite NBA game, baseball game, what have you, and then relax and come home at night and watch it—and choose if you wish to forward through the commercials and just get to the highlights. That's almost impossible now because of mobile and the instant access to Twitter and other means of social media.

"Unless someone is terribly blind or deaf, it precludes any chance to go and rewatch a game safely. You almost now have to have a live environment."

Mobile as the First Screen

Some have dubbed mobile the "third screen." Kosner isn't in that camp. He thinks mobile is much more.

"I fundamentally believe that mobile, and I'm including tablets here, is the first screen for consumers and is going to be the first screen for sports fans if it's not readily apparently already," he says. "This is not like a little extension technology. This is not like a brand extension or a sub-brand. This is prime time. This is where people are starting their days. This is where people are ending their days.

"The functionality that is possible and coming is off the charts and the conventional wisdom that fans wouldn't watch video on their phones or wouldn't be receptive to advertising has all been proven wrong."

How a Marketer Might Look at ESPN

As detailed, ESPN has many products and more content than a media planner can review. Some marketers buy across properties like the World Cup. Others are driven by device preference.

"Obviously you have a choice," Kosner says. "Our thought is to provide the best content experience for fans on their best available screen, which increasingly is mobile and is increasingly more than one device at a time. You could be sitting watching your big-screen TV and also watching another game on your tablet interacting with fans or setting a fantasy lineup on your phone. We have packages where a marketer would buy a particular device but increasingly the power is that we exist on more than one screen, we have scale, and whether it's the World Cup or the BCS [College Football Bowl Championship Series] or our Gamecast, it's a differentiated product from others that are out there."

While at Yahoo!, Bayle built a global team that created mobile campaigns for Fortune 500 partners in 29 markets. He believes that time and better mobile experiences make the selling job easier today.

"Frankly speaking, I see some improvements from pioneering the space if you will with Yahoo! Mobile," he says. "In many cases, our sales teams were the first to speak to agencies presenting opportunities in what we called the display format or the more digitally paralyzed format versus what had whet the appetites of some marketers prior to that—the use of SMS [short message service] and other means that are truly mobile specific.

"I still see some frozen faces in meetings where sadly that's the first time that the agency had experimented or understood including the investment of dollars in a display-based means of what mobile can allow for them. A change from 2007 to [20]12 is the advent of the display format being fully multimedia rich and obviously rich media being paramount and at the forefront of what you can do creatively. The one critical reaction that agencies had in 2007 that was an excuse on why they didn't invest was, 'I can't tell a story; I can't build a brand there.' You never hear that now—that has completely evaporated."

Bayle doesn't blame it all on the marketers.

"We were very myopic at the outset as an industry in suggesting, 'Okay, we have this thing called BlackBerry, we have this thing called iPhone,'" he says. "That paid homage to the content-based guys who came out of the gates and tried to repurpose their content.

"To really go back and peel the onion to what a marketer wants, they want to reach the right audience at the right time. It should be inconsequential how they accomplish that goal. There are some circumstances that don't fit this equation but for the most part, if I'm a CPG [consumer product goods] marketer, I'm automotive, I'm in a travel-based category, let's make it simple for them to reach that fan base no matter whether the fan base is using a tablet, using an iPad, or using a BlackBerry. "We're very careful to ensure that we leave the message that you can reach a large leading category through ESPN across a multitude of devices and we work very closely with the agencies to have them appreciate how to have the right orientation from a production standpoint and ad creative standpoint. We can contribute to that cause so the marketer can get that ubiquity from our fans spending time across all these devices."

Giving Fans Their Fill

Kosner isn't a sports lifer but he's darn close. A three-decade veteran of sports media, he began his tenure at the network in 1997 as vice president of programming development for ESPN. Prior to ESPN, Kosner worked at CBS Sports, the NBA (where he headed up the league's broadcasting department for seven years), and Sports Illustrated, where he developed television and interactive programming for *Sports Illustrated* and *SI for Kids* magazines.

It seemed right to ask him if we've reached the point where fans no longer have the time, appetite, or means to consume more.

"I don't think we're even close," Kosner says. "Steven Bornstein, who now runs all media at the NFL [National Football League] and was the president of ESPN and the guy who hired me 16 years ago, told me that every time you think you've satisfied the fans, you realize that you've underestimated the level of interest.

"Where I see this going is higher and higher degrees of personalization and customization. We do something cool like with our alerts, for instance—we allow you now to set alerts for just a game or just a quarter of a game. You don't have to necessarily subscribe to alerts as a season subscription. I see the ability of people to spin up individual sessions with each other—you see this with Google Plus Hangouts for instance—I see the degree of personalization built upon your interests, the interests of your fans, what you're doing at the moment, to get more and more profound. We started with ESPN.com which is a website that you went to and everybody had exactly the same experience. There was some hierarchical navigation and now we're moving into dynamic touch experiences on any number of devices.

"What's exciting to me is we're just scratching the surface. That extends into the advertising experience and what's possible in marketing. If you look at what's coming with near field communication and daily deals and the advent of digital currencies like iTunes and Amazon Prime, there's a revolution in the content and commerce experience. All that is going to be driven by mobile devices."

Bayle agrees with his boss on the question of whether the fan is filled to the brim.

"For certain, the sky is the limit," he says. "I think it would [take] a pessimist to say everything we'll see has been invented already. That carries very much through here. The company historically has been a leader in things like programming the first 3D-based content—that may even carry through to mobile."

ESPN and the Mobile/Social Convergence

Bayle, who has been in mobile so long that some consider him a lifer, believes that social, mobile, and the fan are forever linked.

"Social is critical to be successful in as much as fans by nature will be social, either touting or taunting their friends or loved ones or even finding new friends just by the nature of how people rally around teams so to speak," he says. "I think there's a concept here . . . the concept of the 'game around the game.'"

Bayle sees more interaction between fans and ESPN personalities, providing more opportunities for marketers to be part of the bond that only sports bring.

"The goal with our mobile teams is to improve the access to fans and to real-time interact with that content," he says.

Other Statistics Provided by ESPN to Show Mobile's Expanded Role

- On weekends during Fantasy Football season, activity on mobile is four times that of access through personal computer.
- The app for ESPN The Magazine is most read on Saturday mornings.
- Tablets account for 11 percent of ESPN's mobile traffic.
- The top advertiser categories for ESPN wireless properties are automotive, insurance, beer, and movie studios.

The "Remote Control for Life"

If "This is the Year of Mobile" had become a cliché, so, too, was the claim made by some in the industry that the mobile device had become "the remote control for life."

Yes, consumers were relying on their cell phones to wake them, entertain them, inform them, and connect them, but it was pure hype to say that mobile subscribers needed but one tool to manage everything.

Then we met a girl named Siri.

Introduced in October 2011 as the signature feature in Apple's iPhone 4S, Siri delivered device owners suggestions, recommendations, and assistance through voice recognition. Siri was marketed as the smart helper that gets things done. All we have to do is ask.

There are obvious benefits to having an electronic concierge to help us manage our lives and work—if the technology works, of course. However, there are drawbacks. Voice recognition is not entirely suited to how we live our lives. There are times when you can't speak out loud (in class or during a play to name two). And let's not forget that voice recognition has been inexact for years, especially in loud places where the technology often can't distinguish one voice or noise from another.

There are huge implications for brands when our personal devices are equipped with personal digital assistants. Are companies going to continue to pay for an ad in a Google query if a mobile subscriber can bypass traditional keyword search altogether by just asking his or her new and knowledgeable pal, Siri? Will advertisers still sponsor the traffic alerts if Siri can tell their customers all they need to know? (As of early 2012, Siri was not providing live traffic updates.)

On the positive side, the concierge concept could deliver market- ers deeper demographics and more insights into what people want, prefer, and demand based on what they ask Siri to do in the first place. Siri may be the next big thing, but only time, not Siri, will tell.

Frank Barbieri, senior vice president of emerging platforms for Silicon Valley–based YuMe, says Siri is a step forward but not the end- all killer app.

"Voice is being used as a navigational and utility tool," he says. "What Siri does is bring great utility to navigate an experience. Because we're a car-based culture, voice commands will take off and always have a place, but when people are in close confined places, people feel weird talking to a phone. They would much rather just tap it out."

29

Looking Internationally for Guidance

THE INTERNATIONAL INFLUENCE ON the wireless industry is profound and complex. A look at each market could fill another book, given the differences as well as the nuances.

The commonality is that consumers and merchants worldwide are using mobile in personal and relevant ways. Also, you would be hard-pressed to find a locale where wireless is moving backward rather than steaming forward.

In 2010 a United Nations' study on sanitation reported that far more people in India have access to a mobile phone than to a toilet. A year later, Nielsen reported that in Africa more people can get their hands on a wireless device than clean drinking water.

Among the most fascinating mobile evolutions is in the area of the so-called unbanked, those who never have had access to money services and those living on less than $2 a day.

The GSMA Mobile Money for the Unbanked program (MMU) was launched in 2009 supported by worldwide mobile operators as well as a grant from the Bill & Melinda Gates Foundation. The program's goal was to reach 20 million people in remote areas such as Papua New Guinea, Bangladesh, El Salvador, and Mozambique by 2012.

"When you think about Asia, every country is different," says Michael Becker, Mobile Marketing Association North America managing director. "For instance, in India, they are worried about scale because their systems are taking on so many new customers so quickly. We can definitely learn about scale. The likes of Japan and Korea, we can learn about the likes of next-generation services and commerce.

"From a developing market such as Bangladesh, we're going to learn about how to use the lowest common denominator to deliver the greatest amount of value. We can learn what it means to engage with the previously unbanked. This whole world of consumers who have never banked before and now what does it mean that they can [bank] with their mobile device? The rawness of those experience can be used to develop really focused experiences for us in North America."

Restrictions for U.S. Marketers

Some have criticized the U.S. mobile operators for having such tight controls on messaging. The rules and guidelines, developed in tandem with the Mobile Marketing Association (MMA) and industry players including Hipcricket, are bound in a document that totals more than 150 pages.

Although reading the guide and understanding the rules is a significant task—and one often left to the vendors and those who have tried everything else in a failed attempt at sleeping—the U.S. mobile marketing industry considers the restrictions necessary to avoid such situations as what is happening in India, where mobile users are inundated with short message service (SMS) spam messages.

"Here, there's a lot of chaos as far as SMS marketing is concerned," says Vineet Durani, director of the Windows Phone business group at Microsoft who is based in Gurgaon, India. "Enforcement is struggling around spamming. The user can get up to 100 promotional messages a day. For a brand to be able to stand out is difficult. But there are new heavy fines for brands that don't follow the rules of privacy. Microsoft follows its global privacy policies and SMS campaigns have been very, very successful for us."

Beyond texting, the fervor for social networking has hit India, where even feature phones retailing below $50 have a Facebook button and a first year of unlimited Facebook service available for free.

The great majority of mobile users in India buy prepaid cell phone plans. As for content, the three most popular topics, according to Durani, are astrology, cricket, and the film industry known as Bollywood and based in Mumbai.

Learning by Observing

Some read books like this one. Others attend conferences. Benjamin Gauthey, Microsoft's digital marketing lead, Asia and Pacific, learns about mobile by visiting Starbucks, museums, parks, and trains in every city he goes.

With responsibilities in multiple countries, Gauthey spends three or four hours per trip observing wireless users.

He says Singapore is "extremely overwhelming" with mobile prevalent on trains and users playing games and conversing via an American-based application called WhatsApp. Gauthey has found Korea to be home to high-definition video viewing of soap operas and YouTube video.

"Mobile has unique local context," he says. "One size does not fit all."

When Thinking Global, Think Local

In Asia, some of the biggest opportunities to reach consumers are through location-based services.

"Foursquare links the small businesses and the consumer," says Simon Mouyal, Microsoft's cloud marketing lead in Asia Pacific. "There is opportunity here if you have a good value proposition."

Mouyal also sees the cloud becoming more important, especially to those who do not have personal computers. The cloud is defined by Wikipedia as "the delivery of computing as a service rather than a product, whereby shared resources, software, and information are provided to computers and other devices as a utility (like the electricity grid) over a network (typically the Internet)".

More engaged consumers are seeking a home for their content beyond what is possible on a wireless device. In addition, they are seeking to access the content anytime, anywhere, on any computer or mobile.

"You can't put everything on mobile," Mouyal says.

Canada Plays Catch-Up

You would be hard-pressed to find a more savvy Canadian mobile marketer than Jonathan Dunn. Still, Dunn admits that he has had to rely as much on intuition as anything.

"I've argued for some time now that the biggest difference between Canada and the United States when it comes to mobile is marketer spend," says Dunn, associate director for mobile sales and marketing at Bell Media. "We've lacked the same depth of research data that's available in the United States and that's held back marketer investment as the case to divert funds from other channels or release new funds is harder to make. But with comScore now tracking Canadian activity and other recently published findings, we're seeing a lot of similarities between United States and Canadian mobile behavior. Smartphone penetration is comparable. Canadians love to text.

"For the most part, Canadian publishers have done a good job creating mobile assets, and the available data backs up strong consumer adoption. Brand mobile destinations are one area where Canada is lagging. Investments in mobile advertising are also lagging as a share of overall digital budgets, but the growth rates are strong for both display and search. Mobile coupons and robust mobile loyalty programs are beginning to emerge but aren't widespread and probably need a couple of big retail champions to really gain momentum. That said, there are many marketers that have well thought out and supported mobile strategies and sectors like automotive, financial services, and entertainment/media are making substantial investments."

Dunn has seen significant changes in conversations with brands.

"The level of sophistication has certainly increased," he says. "That's to be expected, though. We've gone through many of the same cycles as the U.S. explaining SMS, keywords, short codes, and double opt-ins; mass stampedes toward building apps [applications]; vigorous debate on the merits of apps versus mobile Web; realizing that mobile works best when it's not in a vacuum, and so on. However, for everything that changes, just as much stays the same. The most common conversation with many brands is about the opportunities and benefits of mobile and defining executional best practices.

"For those brands that are making investments in mobile, there is a greater willingness to include testable variables within their campaigns—creative or targeting A/B splits, unique keywords by media in SMS campaigns, etc. Sadly, for every well-executed campaign there are still mobile ads that click to desktop sites or QR [quick response] codes that do the same, which ends in a negative user experience. On the upside, I now see mobile advertising as a specific line item in RFPs [requests for proposals] and though budgets may still be 'experimental' for many advertisers the intent to work in the channel is growing. Currently, I see a couple things that are really top of mind of most brands—clarifying analytics and ROI [return on investment], understanding the role each mobile channel can play within the context of a more unified media strategy, and building the business case for initial or increased investments."

Dunn's measuring stick on mobile marketing extends beyond dollars spent.

"Revenue only tells part of the story," he says. "There are at least a couple of other ways to gauge mobile's momentum. First, from a consumer-facing view, continued growth in smartphone penetration, SMS volume, mobile Web and app traffic, mobile social media use, use of location services and so on all show rapid—and in some cases exponential—adoption of mobile. Marketers' use of available mobile tactics is growing more slowly than consumer adoption, and those consumer indicators are a great measuring stick of mobile's momentum and opportunity.

"The second way involves more anecdotal or observational evidence but it holds water with me. I take note of the number and variety of advertisers running mobile ad campaigns or the frequency with which I encounter brand or publisher mobile websites. I notice instances of SMS- or QR-code-driven calls to action in traditional media. I register traditional campaigns that call out mobile assets. All of these are on the rise and while it's more difficult to quantify, it's there for all to see. If I take a look at my own business, in 2011 we tripled mobile advertising revenue over 2010 and ran over 150 mobile advertising campaigns. Not all of them had major budgets attached to them, but the volume of both new advertisers and repeat advertisers is a clear indicator of a business that's going from strong to stronger."

The Contrasts between Europe and America

Peggy Anne Salz, an American working in Europe as a global wireless commentator and analyst, is fascinated by American mobile advancements.

"I'm amazed at the U.S. growth given the interoperability issues which stunted messaging and the central role of the PC [personal computer] in defining our digital lives," she says. "Europe may not be where all the action is—but it is where the opportunity is. I live in Germany—considered to be the sleeping giant of mobile. Boy, it will be exciting to see the impact firsthand. Predictably, Europe's growth opportunities are as diverse as its geography."

Would American marketers be wise to study European mobile practices?

"Yep," Salz says. "Europe has made great strides doing pretty basic things like messaging. It has overcome interoperability issues that still plague operators in the United States and elsewhere. It has gotten tremendous mileage out of messaging. It has seen local brands with local content, products, and offers get involved in mobile and reap impressive results.

"Now it is innovating in other messaging services such as IP-based group messaging that surely signal a new chapter in the evolution of how we communicate and lead our truly digital lives. Mobile marketing is effective—despite divides between cultures, countries, and languages. Europeans know how to create compelling messages for diverse audiences and devices and drive results."

Salz is always on the lookout for technology that changes the norm.

"Europe has also given birth to a new breed of IP-based messaging services that are exciting and disruptive," she says. "The outcome: a slew of applications that enable one-to-many messaging. In practice these allow users to create or add groups, and send messages out to those who join the group. Thus, one-to-many broadcast models are springing up and entire communities are forming around messaging using these applications. The drivers? First, the move to open operating systems for mobile devices, making it possible for developers to create applications for Android-based devices, for example. Second, increasing availability of ubiquitous high-speed mobile data networks and Wi-Fi. This presents an opportunity for start-up companies to develop and distribute applications that enable over-the-top services."

Philippe Poutonnet, a Frenchman working for Hipcricket in the United States, has been in mobile for more than a decade beginning as an industry analyst.

"The United States has caught up with Europe," he says. "Five years ago, Europe was ahead of the United States in interoperability, in mobile data services, adoption, wireless penetration, in handset manufacturers with Nokia leading the way. Now the game has totally changed. The picture is 180 degrees different.

"The United States is now ahead of Europe in hardware and software, Android, iOS, ahead of the game in mobile advertising. Advertising in the United States is far superior in terms of consumption. When it comes to Super Bowl advertising, nothing else like that exists in the rest of the world."

Mario Schulzke, an international marketer who spends half the year in Europe and the other half in the States, shares Poutonnet's perspective.

"Marketing and specifically advertising is still a bit more respected in Europe," he says. "That's partially because it's looked at as a craft and because governments are regulating out the super sleazy crap.

"That being said, the innovation is happening in the United States," he adds.

And so is the growth.

According to wireless analyst Chetan Sharma, the U.S. wireless data market grew 5 percent quarter over quarter and 21 percent year over year to reach $17 billion in mobile data service revenues in the third quarter of 2011 and was on course to increase year over year by 22 percent to $67 billion in 2011.

Smartphones continued to be sold at a brisk pace, accounting for 57 percent of the devices sold in 2011's third quarter.

"The feature phone as a device species is on the verge of extinction," Sharma says.

Latin America—One Size Does Not Fit All

To understand the mobile landscape in Latin America is to know that the region is not homogenous—and not easily comparable to the United States.

"I could say the similarities and differences between both markets is defined by the whole economic structure in the region, defined by a well-educated elite with access to the newest devices and trends—and best services—and the remaining low-middle to lower classes with very limited access and nondigitally native," says Terence Reis, director of operations/partner at Pontomobi Interactive and a former Mobile Marketing Association managing director.

"If you're in Sao Paulo [Brazil] you would be led to believe that we have more similarities—you'll find in the richer neighborhoods iPhones, Androids, and BlackBerrys everywhere, people discussing and downloading apps, their heads merged within the screens of their devices. This is reflected on a surge of demand from ad agencies and brands of apps for their services, products, and campaigns.

"However, if you look closer, you'll see that this is only a small share of the market—currently around 15 percent more or less of subscribers."

Like every region in the world, cost is a big factor in the rate of adoption.

"Of course, as all trends, it only tends to move forward," Reis says. "As of last year, the mobile Web access was limited by expensive data pricing—and all carriers have started to push their prices lower and lower, resulting in a 7 [times] growth for many publishers on their mobile Web page views.

"It's likely we'll find a ceiling—80 percent plus of subscribers in the region, varying between countries from 70 percent to 90 percent, are prepaid users, with a low ARPU [average revenue per user], and a rigid one, meaning a growth on any service would mean a decrease in another. This ceiling can always be circumvented—it's a matter of how creative carriers can become. We already have plans offering access only to social networks."

Reis says the mobile advancements often begin in his home country.

"Of course, [Latin America] is a big region," he says. "Usually you'll see these trends starting in Brazil and moving toward Argentina, Mexico, Chile, Venezuela, Colombia—the other countries in the region offering a more sophisticated usage.

"Mobile Web, mobile apps, a convergence between mobile and social networks, services moving to mobile, you can find all of these around the region, with a gap that I'd say of some 18 months to 24 months from most advanced regions. And then you have a big population relying on prepaid usage, whose services are still mostly voice and SMS. How big is that usage? Well, really not as big as any other region—advanced or not."

Big in other regions, including Asia and the United States, texting lags in Latin America.

"The biggest users such as Argentina will send an average of 150 SMS a month," he says. "A month. Just try and compare this to the Philippines. Or your standard U.S. teen. In Brazil we're still below 50 SMS a month. Price is the main culprit—an SMS in Brazil costs some two (U.S.) cents. This for a country with a per capita revenue many times lower than the United States. But education could as well be guilty of constraining a higher usage—not only of SMS but also of mobile Web services.

"All over the region you'll find a very interesting stat: the number of subscribers is much bigger than the number of adequately literate adults. And we could say literacy has a direct impact on the proper usage of digital services. As a result, the use of value-added services— although an important market—is still limited in its numbers, never reaching more than 10 million subscribers a year in Brazil, for instance. So, big difference here—the image of users sending SMS incessantly is hardly a common feature on the biggest part of the market. These users being almost always the same users that we have identified as the smartphone users and app downloaders.

Reis breaks down mobile marketing in Latin America by product and service.

"With SMS, rules vary between countries," he says. "You have in Mexico, Argentina, and Venezuela stronger and more easily accessible business models to marketers, which means you'll see SMS and content bundles and a bigger number of SMS promotions than in Brazil. The usage of SMS as a channel for brands is also more readily available.

"In the case of Brazil you have complicated rules and sometimes expensive business models, constraining the overall usage of SMS by marketers."

And then there is the mobile Web and applications.

"This is a market that has been growing for the last 12 to 18 months," Reis says. "In countries such as Venezuela and Colombia you'll see an interesting access to the mobile Web, probably due to the popularity of BlackBerrys in these countries.

"Mexico has an interesting mobile Web ecosystem. In Brazil the mobile Web is still limited to the big publishers such as UOL, Terra,

Yahoo! with almost no content available from midtier publishers and very far from having a long tail. Argentina still lags behind in these markets.

Reis says social products and services have factored into mobile's progress.

"Conversations with brands have been changed more by the spread of social networks than by anything," he says. "The sense of entitlement and the urge for a more immediate answer—and a straight answer, not the standard marketer talk—have been big drivers of the public attitude.

"Brands have been slow to adopt the mobile channel as a way to deliver better conversations—which is a pity, as the mobile is uniquely positioned to deliver what the public expects from them. Apps have been poorly adapted to legacy customer care systems and seldom integrated to brand metrics. SMS is still randomly used, with services such as banks, airlines, laboratories, and now utilities being the main adopters."

Reis does not judge mobile's movement by the money spent by marketers.

"I have always said that the year of mobile will be the year people stopped asking this silly question," he says. "And it wouldn't be a case of generating revenues, but of how pervasive and transparent would be the adoption of mobile services, products, etc.

"I'd say that the better gauge is the fact we've moved away from being part of the tech sections to the lifestyle section of blogs, papers, TVs, etc. Mobile is part of the daily life of many users and this is the best way to feel satisfied about our momentum in [Latin America]. Unfortunately this also means there's an enormous gap between users' adoption and marketers'."

How Microsoft Handles Disparate Markets

Mobile's variances are especially pronounced for Microsoft's Barbara Williams, whose job is to bring consistent best practices to all regions of the world.

"There is a ton of disparity, and for Microsoft it's not only country to country, it's business group to business group and product to product," she says. "With my role being at the center of all of it, I was just in a meeting today looking at a mobile measurement framework and creating one, I have to look at it at the highest possible level. That it has enough detail to make it actionable for all the different marketers, but it also has to be broad enough to cover all of the different scenarios.

"The ecosystem, whether it's SMS or mobile Web, is different in almost every country and in some cases in the region it's different. How you execute with the privacy laws and what's relevant to people in those particular markets changes. We in most cases are selling products that take more consideration than if you're buying a Coca-Cola or some other personal type product. We look up and down the funnel across all types of tactics and viewpoints depending on what audience and part of the planet you are."

30

Hipcricket Builds for the Future

By the beginning of 2011, Hipcricket had hit its stride. The company's pace of activity had steadily advanced since the company powered its first campaign in 2004. Hipcricket developed and executed 17,000 campaigns in the first half of 2010 and nearly doubled that number in the first six months of 2011, attesting in part to mobile's progress and clients who viewed the channel as an ongoing consumer relationship tool rather than a means to run one-off programs. By the middle of the year, the company was recording double-digit percentage month-over-month growth in the number of campaigns processed each month.

In addition, Hipcricket's mobile advertising solutions had been utilized by companies in more than 15 industries, with a particular focus on quick-service restaurants (QSR), retail, travel, technology, and consumer packaged goods (CPG).

"Certainly positioning ourselves beyond a technology company has helped Hipcricket immensely," says Doug Stovall, senior vice president of sales and client services. "Strategically we talked about it but then we got some very large customers that used us for every mobile marketing channel out there and as a result we could say, 'Look we've done it, we are a full-service company.' It's candidly why we're exploding now—we do everything and we do it well.

"We want to have that mentality that when a customer comes to us and says, 'Hey, can you do this?' we make sure we can or that there's a clear path to getting something done. We want to have the 'can do' attitude at Hipcricket. We want our customers to come at us with stuff that they've never tried before but that we've done with other customers or things that no one has ever tried before. I certainly personally have that mentality and as a company we have that mentality.

"We try to be honest. We think that helps us sell more. We don't want one campaign. We don't want a six-month relationship. We want a many-year relationship with our customers."

By 2011, Hipcricket was again privately held. Its success caught the attention of many suitors, some looking to invest in the business and others exploring a possible acquisition.

"There were multiple avenues that we were examining," company president Ivan Braiker says. "It was a time that we all knew that mobile was going to grow at a more rapid pace and the need for more resources was definitely going to be there. We looked at the ability to raise more financing and do another [financing] round and had multiple discussions on that. Through those discussions, there were overtures from several different companies about merging or acquiring us.

"Our team had several discussions. The talk of a rollup [of synergistic entities] in the mobile industry has been going on for a couple of years. Everybody knew it was going to happen and just didn't know what the timing was going to be. We even had some discussions with some of the venture players and investors about those types of things. Nobody was quite comfortable yet doing that."

The talks with Augme Technologies, a public company with valuable patents and other intellectual property if not a brand as well known as Hipcricket's, began in the spring of 2011.

"When the door opened up in the discussions with Augme, there were multiple things going on," Braiker says. "First, as an overall company, it was a really good fit. You [Augme] weren't just buying [Hipcricket's] revenue, you were buying [Hipcricket's] technology. When you looked at the technology, it was a very good marriage. Hipcricket had built a very powerful state-of-the-state SMS [short message service] platform with state of the art analytics, CRM [customer relationship management] and all that you really needed to do the things we were focusing on doing. And we had some trusted partners we were bringing in for some of the other elements we needed. Some of those elements are what Augme brought to the table."

Augme's AD LIFE™ mobile marketing technology platform had been using patented device-detection and proprietary mobile content adaptation software to solve the mobile marketing industry problem of disparate operating systems, device types, and on-screen mobile content rendering. The patents were considered foundational in the areas of targeted content for the Internet and mobile advertising as well as mobile device detection and content targeting and target marketing.

"They had created a state-of-the-state mobile Web platform along with QR [quick response] codes and integration," Braiker says. "The two companies coming together really did give you a 'soup to nuts' ability. When it came to the focus of the verticals we were going after, with our strength being broadcast, QSR [quick service restaurants] and CPG [consumer packaged goods], a lot of where Augme was coming from was a very strong position in health care and pharmaceuticals, which was a vertical we really even hadn't gone after at Hipcricket."

The discussions got more serious with Augme chief executive officer (CEO) and chairman Paul Arena in part because Augme and Hipcricket had determined that a combined entity would have little overlap.

"As both companies were doing their due diligence, you could see that there were no conflicts," Braiker says. "As you looked at our [sales] pipelines, I don't think we had two potential clients in common. It just seemed to make sense. They were a public company, they had an incredible IP portfolio with patents that if you look through you see that almost anybody playing in the mobile Web space today is infringing on. At a point in time, we'll see how all of that plays out. We believe in an unqualifying way that they are all infringing.

"When you put that together, we believed we would be the leader in the United States, which we are. You look at the client portfolio that the two companies [have]. There isn't anybody who can show the kind of pedigree of clients that our two companies do, now as one. Paul Arena not only came from a substantial Wall Street background, he had also been the driver of two technology companies that had become worth a lot of money [Geos Communications, formerly i2

Telecom International, and Cereus, which became a NASDAQ-listed public company that achieved a market capitalization in excess of $350 million]. He understands that side of the business. Not only does he understand IP, he understands how you do that on Wall Street."

Understandably, Arena viewed the possible acquisition as a means to bring additional shareholder value.

"What interested us the most about Hipcricket was the company's coolness, mobile marketing capabilities, talented employees, and culture," Arena says. "We saw an ability to create the largest mobile marketing company in the United States with the leading best practices, mobile marketing SaaS [software as a service] platform, plus full CRM integration on an API architecture, more experience in deliverables, over 130,000 mobile campaigns, and tracking and analytics capabilities."

The deal was consummated in the summer of 2011 with Arena remaining the CEO and chairman of the larger organization, Braiker becoming president, Eric Harber being named chief operating officer and Tom Virgin becoming chief financial officer. In addition, Stovall headed the larger organization's sales and client services and I was named chief marketing officer.

The combined companies' client roster totaled more than 300 and included:

- Ten of the world's top 20 pharmaceutical companies
- Six of the largest media companies in the world
- Four of the largest advertising agencies in the world
- Three of the leading quick-service restaurant groups in the world
- One of the largest food companies in the world

The purchase price of $44.5 million was composed of $3 million in cash, a $1 million promissory note, $2 million to be paid to holders of Hipcricket options (which amount Augme could pay, at its discretion, in either cash or Augme's common stock), and $38.5 million in Augme's common stock. In addition, the transaction called for a 12-month earn-out payment to Hipcricket shareholders and employees valued at up to an additional $27.5 million, which may be paid in cash or Augme's common stock at Augme's discretion provided that the transaction remains a tax-free reorganization.

Augme retained all of Hipcricket's employees, and the Hipcricket team services Hipcricket's customers. By the fall, Augme was selling its products and services exclusively under the Hipcricket brand.

"New customers feel that they must get in the mobile marketing game and catch up," Arena says. "We give them a competitive advantage by shortening the time to market."

In the constantly morphing world of mobile, Braiker had little time to reflect.

"You put eight years behind something, something you thought was going to take about three years . . . it was starting a new industry, not just starting a new business," he says. "Hipcricket was at the forefront of what mobile marketing was going to be in the United States, which is very different from what it is in the rest of the world. The cofounders all share a sense of great pride. All of us are very pleased with what has happened and where it's going. It's not over. I feel lucky to still be involved and to still be a key driver to the business.

"I don't think any of us are taking a breath. I wish we were but we are not. We're all driven to build a premier mobile company and maintaining what it is and continuing to grow the leadership in the industry. All of us have a pretty high profile that is great for the company. We intend to continue to help lead the industry not only from our marketing aspect but also from our technology. We have some great leaders in our technology department that are keeping us in the forefront."

Tom Virgin, chief financial officer, sees the larger entity as an influential force.

"The advantage of combining the companies was bigger girth—we have 135 people (at the time of the sale), we more than doubled the size," says Virgin. "And we had better access to the capital markets with Augme being publicly traded. It strengthened the balance sheet of Hipcricket. Paul is a great addition to the team.

"Integration is always challenging. What's nice is sometimes you put companies together and you don't actually like the people on the other side. I think we all like the people from Augme. They are nice people like us. They are nice to be around and they're friendly. They're outgoing and they want to be successful as well. Sometimes you don't have that. It's very satisfying. For me and for many people who do the sorts of things we do, it's 'Do you like the team you're working with?' and 'Is it intellectually challenging?' Those were all things that were here."

Harber views the deal as a winner for Hipcricket clients as well.

"It provides the market with the preeminent provider of end-to-end mobile marketing and mobile advertising solutions company," he says. "There have been specialist mobile marketing companies, even subspecialists mobile messaging SMS companies. You've had companies that have done mobile Web, mobile application, more advertising. That is a mess for brands.

"MillerCoors is a huge company with tons of reach and sophistication and complexity. But they don't want all of that [mobile industry fragmentation]. It's way too complicated. Give them end-to-end service from strategy in the beginning to the solutions that deliver on the promises made during the strategy to execute against their need. And then have the systems to measure that and to see if you're doing what you said you would do. Provide those results, optimize, make changes to improve. Then work that cycle over and over again."

Like his colleagues, Harber was gratified.

"It's certainly very personally rewarding," he says. "It has been a long journey, over four years working at it. This company was early in mobile marketing and mobile advertising, in the early stage of doing the evangelism and building the market. I fundamentally believe that Hipcricket is one of the companies that built the market. In one sense, it's just the conclusion of one chapter that was really exciting. It was a great outcome—great price for Hipcricket, great value for the acquirer and for us as the acquired firm, but then it's on to the next chapter."

In October 2011, the global wireless analyst firm Frost & Sullivan said Hipcricket "has emerged as the preferred provider of high-impact mobile marketing solutions in the United States" and "its recent acquisition by Augme Technologies is expected to further consolidate the company's position as an industry powerhouse." Frost & Sullivan recognized Hipcricket with the North American Customer Value Enhancement Award.

Vikrant Gandhi, a senior analyst with Frost & Sullivan, said, "Key reasons for [Hipcricket's] strong performance include strength of its product portfolio, strong service and support capabilities, exceptional speed of execution, and overall strategic acumen of its leadership team.

"Hipcricket is a unique company that has successfully adopted a full-service approach to help marketers understand and leverage the potential of mobile marketing. Frost & Sullivan believes that

Hipcricket is poised for continued success in the U.S. mobile marketing and advertising markets, and presents the company with the 2011 Customer Value Enhancement Award in recognition of its ability to deliver the best results to its customers and partners."

Gandhi forecast a bright future.

"Hipcricket continues to invest in appropriate technologies and systems to offer innovative, next-generation, and integrated mobile marketing and advertising solutions," said Gandhi. "Its recent acquisition by Augme Technologies is expected to further consolidate the company's position as an industry powerhouse in mobile marketing.

"Frost & Sullivan opines that the combined Hipcricket-Augme entity will have one of the most innovative and complete sets of mobile marketing and advertising solutions in the industry. This will enable the company to realize its vision of providing end-to-end service and support to mobile marketers. With Hipcricket's management retaining the key positions at the new entity, Frost & Sullivan expects that Hipcricket will continue to exceed performance expectations in the coming months and years."

PART III

The Future

AN EXAMINATION OF WHAT might be ahead and the importance of not spending ahead of consumer adoption.

"You have to put on a flak jacket and get a little more risk averse."
—Hank Wasiak, *former vice chairman*
of McCann Erickson WorldGroup, and cofounder
of The Concept Farm

31

Determining Whether Mobile Has Arrived

THE FIRST TIME I heard someone say that "This is the Year of Mobile," I was understandably excited by it. But by 2011, when it was repeated for the sixth straight year, it did nothing more than make me shudder.

It was always my belief that it would be the brands rather than the mobile vendors who would be in position to define the era as such. After all, companies as large as Coca-Cola and as small as the "mom and pop" in Middle America were the ones determining marketing spends and making decisions on whether mobile deserved a piece of the budget.

Try as we might—and did—Hipcricket and others in mobile marketing and advertising could only do so much to drive demand.

By all accounts, the future is bright. The total amount of money spent by U.S. marketers on mobile advertising and promotions will reach about $56.5 billion by 2015, according to Borrell Associates. That expected figure is more than six times the $9.3 billion that was spent on mobile advertising and promotions in 2010.

But whether we reached the tipping point in 2008, 2010, or 2011 or whether 2015 will really be the Year of Mobile is immaterial to those of us who need to accelerate our businesses today.

Much of what has motivated the brands to move, if not jump, into mobile is the need to follow the consumer. And that consumer has become more and more connected, on-the-go, and demanding to maintain a lifestyle that includes social networking even when the personal computer is turned off and left at home.

32

The Ever-Changing Consumer

ACCORDING TO THE PEW Internet & American Life Project, by 2011 cell phones had easily become the most popular device among American adults. Approximately 85 percent of adults owned a cell phone, and 90 percent of all adults—including an astounding 62 percent of those age 75 and older—were living in a household with at least one working cell phone.

Pew found that the device, to use an Apple advertising phrase, *had changed everything*. Specifically:

- Half of all adult cell owners (51 percent) had used their phone at least once to get information they needed right away.
- One quarter (27 percent) said that they had experienced a situation in the previous month in which they had trouble doing something because they did not have their phone at hand.
- Forty percent said they found themselves in an emergency situation in which having their phone with them helped.
- Forty-two percent used their phone for entertainment when they were bored.

Pew's data was in line with what we found through Hipcricket's fourth annual survey that was conducted in the fall of 2011. The company learned that mobile retail websites had emerged as an indispensible in-store tool for consumers as they shop. The questioning revealed that consumers—particularly smartphone owners—were turning to mobile retail sites as a critical tool for locating the products they want, searching for coupons and special discounts, and comparing prices at competitors' stores.

According to the survey, 63 percent of smartphone users had visited a retailer's website from their mobile device—up from 53 percent in 2010—and 41 percent had done so while in the retail store. Of particular interest, 50 percent had checked a competitor's mobile website while in another store.

The research also found that smartphone owners were visiting mobile retail sites to research prices (46 percent); search for coupons and offers (36 percent); research products (28 percent); and purchase products (13 percent).

In general, consumers were finding more value in the mobile Web. Seventy percent of all smartphone users regularly had used their phone to access the mobile Web, second only to short message service (SMS)/texting among data usage on mobile devices.

Hipcricket also found that 33 percent of cell phones users were interested in receiving offers based on time and location—for example, a coupon delivered at 4 PM for $5 off a pizza at a local shop that night only.

Hipcricket's 2010 survey had revealed consumers' interest in being social on their devices. Among the findings: 57 percent of consumers would be interested in opting in to a brand's loyalty club via a mobile social networking application such as Facebook.

33

The Tools You Can Use

Considering Mobile Products and Services Individually

Once you decide that mobile belongs in your plan and you determine your strategy, choosing the tactical elements becomes some of the most important decisions to make. Let's look at the most popular mobile products and services. Each should be considered, but all have limitations (we promised that this book wouldn't be built on hype) to be weighed against potential benefits.

Messaging

I've spent considerable time chronicling the rise of short message service (SMS)/text messaging and providing best use cases. By now you've figured out that if you go the messaging route, you're unlikely to win a major award for innovation. However, if producing business results is your sole mission, SMS deserves to be near the top of your consideration list.

Consider the following:

According to stats provided by CTIA–The Wireless Association, 33 million texts were sent and received in the United States in June 2001. Ten years later, that total was 197 billion. The tipping point came in 2009, when, for the first time, there were more texts sent and received daily than calls made.

Yes, we're still hearing naysayers claim that SMS is a young person's activity only, but as you've seen in *Mobilized Marketing* and elsewhere, texting programs have been successful reaching all demographics.

As an example, here's how to look at SMS if your customer or prospect is a luxury shopper:

- Use SMS as a customer relationship marketing tool, not just a means to provide one-time offers.
- Use past experiences with the customer to offer luxury customers what they actually want.
- Do not assume all luxury customers have smartphones—SMS needs to do a lot of the heavy lifting.
- Use SMS for time-sensitive offers and information. Ninety-seven percent of text messages are read within four minutes of delivery.
- Consider location to boost relevance.
- Make sure SMS campaigns fit into the brand's overall marketing strategy.
- Use SMS as a means to connect to, pardon the pun, richer brand experiences. For example, link back to the brand's mobile website or app.
- For this audience, overdeliver on customer service—it is more of an expectation.
- Use SMS to drive customers to the store.
- Exclusivity is important because it makes customers feel like VIPs, so reward the brand's best customers with something special.

Within the messaging bucket is MMS, or multimedia messaging service. Newer to the scene and not nearly as popular despite the capability being embedded on approximately 200 million phones as of 2011, MMS is a message sent that contains multimedia objects, which may include high-resolution video, motion graphics, a slide show, and more. The message can include customized dynamic content, including unique identifiers such as two-dimensional bar codes.

It can also have an actionable link directing customers to coupons, maps to nearby retail locations, mobile-optimized websites for immediate purchases, or to social media destinations to further your brand mission.

As you consider MMS, it's important to find a provider that will not penalize your brand and the smartphone user by sending multimedia of the lowest common denominator adapted for feature phones. Instead, turn to an entity like Hipcricket that has a device recognition process to ensure content adaptation delivers the best experience.

Also, it is prudent to align yourself with a company that has a robust platform capable of integration to your database or customer relationship management (CRM) platform.

Mobile Web

There are some nice to haves and some musts when considering mobile strategies and tactics. The mobile Web is in the latter category. Why? It's where much of the action is now and certainly where mobile subscribers are going.

Mary Meeker, a former analyst at Morgan Stanley and now a partner at Kleiner Perkins Caufield & Byers in Silicon Valley, California, predicts that by 2013, more people worldwide will access the Internet on a mobile device than on a personal computer (PC).

As discussed numerous times in this book, mobile users aren't looking to duplicate the PC experience. Instead, when it comes to the mobile Web, they are predominantly interested in such quick bites as store hours, nutritional information, and directions. They rarely, if ever, will turn to a mobile phone to delve deeply into a company's 8K or other financial filings.

By the fall of 2011, 43 percent of U.S. mobile subscribers had used a browser, an increase of nearly 3 percent over the June 2001 figure, according to research firm comScore.

Mobile Advertising

As defined by the Mobile Marketing Association, mobile advertising is any collection of text, graphics, or multimedia content displayed and accessible inside of an application for the purposes of promoting a commercial brand, product, or service.

By June 2011, 28 percent of smartphone owners said they had seen an ad on the mobile Web or in an application, according to comScore. Further, 8 percent of smartphone owners and 4 percent of feature phone users had responded to an SMS ad.

Those numbers become more significant if you build your program for consumer activity well beyond a one-time response. Companies, including HBO, have begun with mobile advertising on Hipcricket's network, then invited participating consumers to take part in a VIP club.

In 2009, HBO used mobile ads to raise awareness, primarily among Spanish-speaking Hispanics, for pay-per-view purchases of a boxing match involving Floyd Mayweather Jr. and Juan Manuel Marquez. Consumers were encouraged to text the keyword *Pelea* ("fight" in Spanish) to a short code for a chance to win a signed boxing glove. Those who participated received an SMS message back confirming their entry into the contest and inviting them to join the VIP club.

The campaign generated a whopping 12.9 percent click-through rate, and of those, nearly 70 percent opted in to the SMS club, giving HBO a valuable database for remarketing purposes.

"This is my mantra, this post-click engagement," says Eric Harber, Hipcricket's chief operating officer. "I started talking about this a while back before people started talking about it or knew what it meant. Much of advertising was about presenting the consumer with a mobile banner ad on their small device. You clicked on that banner ad and it presented you with something. Not much, frankly. It could be just an expanded ad unit that had the brand's logo bigger than it was before or it could be some sort of lightweight offer or sending someone to a very small landing page for additional information.

"Post-click engagement is about what happens after that click. That's where our platform and approach to the market puts us at a great advantage on behalf of our customers. That's when the relationship can start if you shepherd it well. The post-click piece of it is about reengagement, it's about in a permission-based way, having an ongoing longitudinal relationship with a customer or a prospect. It's about remonetizing."

Harber recognizes that there is additional effort and investment needed, but he is a strong advocate for making that part of many programs.

"At the end of the day, this is about loyalty, this is about making additional money," Harber says. "It also ties into the CRM of the brand. CRM gets pushed all the way to the edge, in the pocket of your consumer. We have the ability to get data into their CRM systems and management resource systems and take data out of them. Figure out what went well, how can we do better, how do you optimize it?"

Of course, mobile advertising goes well beyond banners. Frank Barbieri has built products to reach viewers of videos and to engage gamers.

"With ads in front of video, the size of budgets is fairly small because of the reach numbers but the value is fairly high so advertisers are willing to pay top dollar for those," says Barbieri, senior vice president of emerging platforms for Silicon Valley–based YuMe. "They show great engagement and great brand metrics and brand lift—perception and awareness around those advertisements.

"On the other hand, video in games as interstitial between levels provides massive reach. There's a huge audience. Your effectiveness goes down but vis-à-vis Web effectiveness, it's much higher. We think that's the case because it's a personal device and you have 100 percent share of voice. The screen size is so small, when an ad takes over that screen, it's really impactful. When a viewer isn't expecting to see an ad, your editorial placement needs to be very cautious. You want to benefit the user, not interrupt the user. The best uses are between levels of a game when they want to take a break."

Barbieri says that mobile advertising will become more integral once measurement becomes more sophisticated.

"Mobile advertising is the Baby Huey of the media world," he says, drawing a comparison to a duckling cartoon character from the 1950s. "It's really big but it's not grown up yet. It hasn't grown up yet simply because there is no service that ranks the top apps [applications] independently. It's incredibly hard for a marketer to figure out what real reach is and if they are getting unduplicated reach. In addition, there is no cookie infrastructure. I'm actually shocked that brands are spending so much on mobile [advertising]. Handset manufacturers and carriers are the ones holding back the use of cookies. Without them changing, mobile media will never reach the sophistication of online media."

Mobile Apps

As defined by CTIA–The Wireless Association, mobile applications are downloadable tools, resources, games, social networks, or almost anything that adds a function or feature to a wireless handset that is available for free or for a fee.

The total number of apps in Apple's and Google's stores topped 1 million by late 2011, according to company figures. Apple gets much of the credit for app development and interest, and, through its marketing, made the expression "There's an app for that" part of our lexicon.

In fact, as discussed earlier, two years before Apple's App Store opened in 2008, Google was advancing the concept.

Simply put, apps provide users expressive brand experiences. A marketer can offer up everything from a game to real-time flight status to nutritional information. Many of the most successful applications have utilitarian benefits like how to prepare a dinner for four or the best route across town during rush hour.

The downsides include the need for a mobile user to find an app, then choose to download it, not to mention use the app.

Although some developers and marketers are making money on applications, not everyone is a fan. Hipcricket's Braiker and Y&R's Thom Kennon are among the naysayers.

"What better marketing organization than Apple?" Braiker asks. "They were convincing the world that they needed an app. There are certain instances when apps are wonderful and they're meaningful, but when you look at the statistics, even in the early days, the average app lasted on a phone for less than 10 days [before it was ignored].

"We've always felt that a more foundation approach was appropriate, one of engagement when you could build your tribe, engage your consumer, and give them more reasons to engage. Then, your ability to launch an app is greater because you already have that foundational base and members of your tribe."

Kennon, too, believes the app interest by marketers has frequently been ill-advised.

"What sucks a lot of the oxygen out of the industry the last two to three years is the obsession with apps," he says. "What it has done is focused on a very clear use case—people who want to have the functionality of a website or something like that. They want to have it in their pocket on varying types of phones. Apps have been a little bit of a crutch we've created to control experiences around branded content and functionality. It's fantastic but what has happened is we get what I call these apps ghettos whether you're in the Android ghetto or the smartphone ghetto or the iPhone or iPad ecosystem (and everything outside those platforms and systems fails to reach consumers)."

Kennon sees coming advancements in mobile Web development as a sign that app infatuation will wane.

"What's really started to get me encouraged to break that choke-hold on creativity, on production, on campaign experience ideas on apps, is the opening up of the mobile Web," he says. "The coming time, which can't be more than two or three years away, where everyone has a quote unquote smartphone. With HTML5 [a common presentation structure for the Internet] embraced and integrated as the standard every day more and more that's going to break open the experience and crack open these little use cases and truly make the experiences portable and agnostic to platform or device. We're poised on the edge of some really breakout brand innovation.

"Finally through that door will hopefully come more brand marketers and their budgets. This is the new Web, the new face of interconnectivity. That's a big, big thing."

QR Codes

Another way to provide some mobile users with information and an engaging experience is through quick response (QR) codes or, as they are sometimes called, two-dimensional codes.

Provided that the phone has a QR scanner, either embedded by the handset manufacturer or downloaded by a cell phone owner, mobile subscribers can simply scan a bar code on a product package or magazine ad, for example, and be linked to a website, video, or other rich media.

The technology was first introduced in Japan in the mid-1990s but adoption was held back due to the lack of a standardized scanner and lack of demand by mobile users in North America.

QR codes eventually gained favor in the West in 2010 and became more common in print ads and on point-of-sale materials, billboards, and many products.

Among the questions to consider:

- Are your customers and prospects relatively early adopters?
- Can you make the QR code easily discoverable?
- Is there a compelling reason for someone to engage with your marketing materials?
- Is there a way to measure the results and optimize in real time?
- Can I use QR codes as a springboard to a longer relationship with my target?

As to consumer interest, Scanbuy reported a 400 percent increase in scans in the first nine months of 2011 compared with the same period a year earlier. Also, the company, which has clients including Home Depot and the U.S. Postal Service, saw a six-week campaign net more than 400,000 scans. In 2010 its largest campaign resulted in 65,000 scans.

Location-Based Services

Geo-Fencing

As defined by CTIA–The Wireless Association, location-based services are an information, advertising, or entertainment service that uses the geographical position of a cell phone.

The scenario often offered to sell the concept involves a consumer walking by a Starbucks and getting pinged with an offer. There are a couple of problems with that characterization. First off, it took years for technology to be introduced for this even to be possible. Second, the great majority of device owners are unwilling to enable their device to be identified without restrictions and reached by brands.

On the other hand, brands are having some success in gaining a subscriber's permission to reach out within a certain location or with a defined type of offer.

An example is the 2011 innovative program run by the MillerCoors brand Blue Moon beer that pings opted-in mobile subscribers in 59 airports in the United States. With Hipcricket, MillerCoors created Blue Moon on the Fly, which begins by asking people to opt in by sending an SMS keyword to Blue Moon beer's short code.

When an opted-in user arrives at a participating airport, he or she receives a welcome message, along with directions to the nearest terminal to find a cold Blue Moon beer. The effort was supported with call-to-action table tents in participating airports and via Blue Moon's Facebook page.

"A lot of it is test and scale," says Steve Mura of MillerCoors. "Specifically when it comes to geo-fencing and those other things, what we do is find the right geography, the right alliance, and when I say alliance, we have all these relationships with Major League Baseball local teams, NFL [National Football League] local teams. [We ask] how do we activate those or we have a brand challenge and we're going to work with a certain technology to help us.

"Once we lay out our strategy, what are our goals and objectives, then we continue to build the pipeline where we have ideas or technologies that we think can help us meet our goals and then go ahead and put some money behind it and test it. The key thing for us is we just don't enter into any program without some idea of how this might scale either from a price perspective or from a technology perspective."

Key Takeaways

- The information provided upon arrival in an airport is welcome because the program is permission based.
- Time is often short in airports and no two are the same—directions to finding one's favorite beer serve a purpose.
- Mura tested the program before he considered running it in more airports.

Check-In Services (Or Is It, "Hey, Check Me Out"?)

Forever, it seems, people have sought to tell those in their circle where they are and what they're doing (often without convincing any of us why we should care). Whether it's an attempt to show us how cool they are or to broadcast the fact that they believe that they are having a better time than we are, the activity has gained steam recently through Foursquare's introduction of the "check in."

Launched in 2009 at the hipper-than-hip South by Southwest conference in Austin, Texas, Foursquare has positioned itself for consumers as the ideal way to explore the world around them. Once they checked in via a downloaded mobile application, they could broadcast their status not only to other Foursquare users but also to those in their networks on Facebook and Twitter.

By late 2011 Foursquare had 10 million members, enough for 500,000 merchants to use the service to theoretically grow their businesses.

Participating merchants get access to real-time data about their customers, including total daily check-ins, most recent and frequent visitors, gender breakdown of customers, data on the time of day people check in, and the portion of the business's Foursquare check-ins that are broadcast to Twitter and Facebook.

To me, the most interesting check-in of the summer of 2011 was done by the Pew Research Center. According to Pew, 28 percent of U.S. mobile owners used wireless phones to get directions or recommendations based on their current location. That equaled 23 percent of all adults.

A much smaller number (5 percent of cell phone owners, equaling 4 percent of all adults) used their phones to check in to locations using geo-social services such as Foursquare or Gowalla (which in late 2011 was purchased by Facebook). As you might expect, smartphone owners were especially likely to use these services on their phones.

What should we make of those figures?

Despite the buzz, the check-in numbers call into question the short- and long-term value of Foursquare and the like.

I have the Foursquare iPhone app and twice have told myself to get committed to the activity. But there just hasn't been enough of a pull for me either time.

Near-Field Communications (NFC)

Will Consumers Soon Leave Their Wallets at Home?   Siri, the voice recognition personal digital assistant introduced earlier in the book, may or may not soon tell us to leave our wallets at home. If she doesn't, she will be in the minority. Everyone from Google to Intuit to PayPal to the credit card companies and mobile operators are creating products and services that address what they believe is an inevitability—the mobile phone replacing the wallet as the most indispensible personal accessory.

It certainly won't be easy or happen quickly, for several reasons.

Battery life on smartphones is notoriously poor. Is a consumer really going to leave a wallet at home if there is a chance that the mobile device will run out of juice just when it's time to pay the dinner bill? Consumers won't risk having to wash dishes to make it up to unhappy restaurant owners.

Point-of-sale (POS) systems change out infrequently. They are highly complex, involving security and reliability. Plus, adaptations to POS technology often require extensive employee training.

There is the critical question of how the pie gets split. There was a day when I might've believed that there was enough money for everyone to be satisfied. That was before I experienced firsthand at InfoSpace how disintermediation happens when entities squeeze middlemen for higher margins.

Finally, mobile devices with near field communications (NFC) are not widely available. For years, NFC has been hailed as the technology we need to enable transactions, data exchange, and wireless connections between two devices in proximity to each other.

All of this isn't to say that the concept will go up in smoke.

Large players have been chasing the mobile wallet promise for nearly a decade. In 2004 the 140 NFC Forum was created with members including LG, Nokia, HTC, Motorola, NEC, RIM, Samsung, Sony Ericsson, Toshiba, AT&T, Sprint, Google, Microsoft, PayPal, Visa, MasterCard, American Express, Intel, TI, and Qualcomm, among others. Harmony and pie sharing were promised.

Years later, we're still at the test phase.

In the spring of 2011, Google, Citi, MasterCard, First Data, and Sprint announced and demonstrated Google Wallet, an app that the parties said would make your phone your wallet so you can tap, pay, and save money and time while you shop. For businesses, Google Wallet was heralded as an opportunity to strengthen customer relationships by offering a faster, easier shopping experience with relevant deals, promotions, and loyalty rewards.

Google Wallet was built to work with MasterCard's PayPass network—a merchant POS service that enables consumers to tap to pay.

Separately, we saw the creation of Isis, a mobile commerce joint venture spearheaded by Verizon Wireless, AT&T, and T-Mobile USA. Before it ever reached consumers' phones, Isis modified its strategy by partnering with the credit card companies to expand payment options. The results have yet to bear fruit.

Intuit, a provider of financial management solutions, is among the companies committing considerable resources to the mobile wallet concept.

"I would use the analogy that it's just like 10 or 15 years ago," says Scott Lien, vice president of the mobile innovation group at Intuit. "None of us had GPS [global positioning system] in our car. When you went somewhere, you dug out a paper map or you got on the Web and you printed out the whole MapQuest thing and off you went. Now I don't use a paper map. We all use Google Maps on our phone or we use GPS that's in the car.

"What we've seen is that the device has increasingly gotten more intelligent, and the GPS in my car knows about traffic and can reroute you on the fly. And it knows when you're running low on gas, and tells you, 'Here's a place to get gas.' It's more than a replacement for the paper map. The same applies here."

Money Manager as Much as Wallet   Lien says we should think money manager rather than simple cash replacement.

"It's inevitable that we will use this smart gadget that most of us have in our pocket now and increasingly over time all of us will have it," he says. "First it will be a basic replacement for payments but over time it will gain more and more intelligence. At first there will be early adopters. They do everything on the phone. I think it will be high travelers and people who are in transit a lot. We have all these frequent flier miles and need something to keep track of everything and being right in our pocket is important. And also heavy commuters in major metropolitan cities. There are a lot of taxis and transit authorities that are doing mobile payment mechanisms because there's a great value proposition for them and for the consumer because you don't have to deal with all the cash and reconciling. It's just you tap your phone and go.

"There are many ways that it will add intelligence. It's shocking in this country that there are a lot of people in tough economic shape. Credit card debt is high. Many people are living paycheck to paycheck yet they don't have a good adviser on a daily basis that is helping them make good buying decisions. That could happen in many ways.

Helping them find substitutes—if you want to get a good cup of coffee, you tell them, 'Here's the cheaper, better place and a better way to get it. Hey, you have points sitting there in your frequent flier account that are about to expire and you can monetize that and buy this thing you want to get.' We all have three or four credit cards in our wallet. We can tell them that there's actually a better card to use on this transaction because they're going to get triple points."

Lien has measured expectations for adoption.

"The concept is very simple—harnessing all the data and all the information that is there and putting all of that knowledge in your hand at the point of purchase or point of decision to help you make a better choice," he says. "I don't think we're years away from all that. I think it will start to come slowly and come in pieces the way they came with the iPhone. First there weren't any apps, now there's voice assist and all that. This will come slowly and serve segments of users like the high traveler, high transit user who will start to adapt it very quickly.

"I look at it in stages. Years ago, when I was young, you would sit with your bank statement and you would do a monthly batch of reconciliation. And then it became more of a weekly Saturday morning activity where you would log in to online banking and see where you're at. Now we're going to be where it's real time all the time. As I go, I can see as conditions changes, as mortgage rates change, as the market goes up and I spend more money and I can see where I'm. I'm making these decisions on the fly."

Progress hasn't come soon enough for some, including Y&R's Thom Kennon.

"Every few years you look and say, 'I thought this would be solved by now,'" he says. "It's interesting that it hasn't. I think we're going to see it settled in urban pockets in Asia before it's ever solved here.

"Is this something Google is going to own and how come it hasn't happened yet? Will it be a consortium of banks? I don't know how it's going to work but I do believe in the very near future, we're going to start to think about our phone before our wallet when we leave our house. It's crazy to think that it shouldn't be one in the same. I just don't know who's going to win that and what the monetization might look like."

Kennon believes the technology challenges will be solved before the splits are worked out.

"It's going to take a partner to connect the very difficult dots of the retail channel, the banking system, the user experience, and how that fits into the device and operating system and ecosystem," he says. "There's enough money to be made for all these actors to invest in it and enough convenience and savings for consumers to embrace it."

Philippe Poutennet, Hipcricket's marketing director and a former wireless industry analyst in Paris, France, anticipates more years of jockeying.

"The next challenge the industry has to solve is the payment one," he says. "We've been through a state where we do communication, voice, data, SMS, and MMS. Now we're exchanging information. Now we have to pay for goods and services directly from mobile advertising. This is the missing step.

"PayPal thinks they can win this on its own. Visa thinks it can win this on its own. AT&T thinks it can win this on its own. It will take three or four years until they realize that they need to create some industry standards."

Mobile Video

Ride along a train in South Korea and you are nearly certain to see commuters watching live television on their mobile devices. Through digital multimedia broadcasting, or DMB, mobile subscribers are primarily watching ad-supported news and sports feeds provided free on DMB-capable devices by the country's television broadcasters.

Surveys have shown that the average viewing time is approximately 15 minutes. Advertisers have taken these habits into account and produced 15- to 30-second commercials as opposed to the minute-long spots typical for Korean television.

As discussed earlier in the book, in the United States, everyone from ESPN to Verizon has tried to make live television viewing a go. Judging by the numbers—by June 2011, only 16 million were watching TV or video on mobile devices, according to comScore—it's more of a no-go, at least for now.

Frank Barbieri, who first built mobile products for MSNBC in 1999, believes he knows why.

"I predicted a faster adoption of mobile viewing over the air," says Barbieri, who has led product initiatives at Microsoft, InfoSpace,

Transpera, and now at YuMe in Silicon Valley. "We thought the handheld screen would be the next consuming screen for viewing content. I think that turned out to be wrong. People were not watching over the air.

"In the early days, they were buying content from iTunes [Apple's content store] and putting it on their iPhone. That has changed a little bit but if you look at applications, they trend toward gaming and utility and social and less toward consumption of long-form video content on mobile phones."

Why not the South Korea model?

"There are particular quirks with the Korea experiment that aren't necessarily true in North America," Barbieri says. "One is that it's a heavy commuter-base culture. There's a lot of downtime. North America is more car-based versus public transport. Second, live video mobile services are free. We've never had that. It's always been a subscription-based service. That has kept usage fairly low.

"In the United States, we are moving more toward view on demand because our Web culture is so entrenched here and there is more interest in time shifting and sideloading the content [by transferring data between devices] versus watching over the air."

Multiple studies show that more video is consumed on phones and tablets over Wi-Fi than through mobile operator networks. There are several reasons for this, including the more stable and faster connection delivered via Wi-Fi as well as the absence of worry of going over one's network monthly data limit.

According to Pew research, by August 2011, 54 percent of smartphone users had viewed a video on their device.

For the three-month average period ending June 2011, more than 16 million mobile users in the United States watched TV or video on their mobile phones, as reported by comScore. Males made up a significantly larger percentage of the mobile TV/video viewing audience (61.8 percent) compared with females (38.2 percent). Users ages 24 to 34 accounted for the largest share of viewers by age, representing 31.8 percent of the total mobile TV/video audience, whereas those ages 18 to 24 accounted for 21.9 percent of viewers and the 35- to 44-year-old segment represented 20.6 percent.

34

The Real Questions Marketers Should Ask

How Fast Should I Go? How Much Time and Dollars Should I Devote?

The easy, although not very helpful, answer to the question of how rapidly a marketer should move in mobile is . . . it depends.

For Steve Mura of MillerCoors, it's the speed at which he can sell more beer through the channel. For Nataki Edwards of AARP, it's about having a meaningful presence in the lives of her members and prospects.

"AARP's philosophy is that we really need to be where our members are," says Edwards, the organization's vice president of marketing, digital strategy, and operations. "Our members are in a lot of different places. They are still consuming print publications, they are still watching TV, and those will continue to be part of our media strategy but the adoption of digital on mobile and the Web can't be denied. We made a concerted effort to make sure we had products and services and offerings in all of those channels. Where mobile comes in, it was really the market showing us the adoption of our members and we kept seeing the numbers go up.

"Our strategy has been to meet them everywhere. We're not just going to build apps [applications]. We're going to make sure that for people who don't have smartphones or who aren't interested in downloading apps that they can still get the best AARP experience on any mobile device."

If mobile wasn't the first thought of AARP marketers by late 2011, at the very least it was on their minds and product roadmaps.

"We're not at the stage where we're creating mobile content specifically for the mobile device but it is a factor in all content creation," Edwards says. "As the pages are built for the Web, we think what can and can't be used for mobile, whether it's the image or Flash—all of those things are taken into consideration.

"Right now the idea is to get to parity when you look at other top media companies out there. What are we offering? Are we comparable to them? We are still figuring out the monetization strategy for mobile. We are selling for mobile but our advertisers are a little bit slower in adoption than we are to creation which isn't a bad problem to have because we want to make sure the products work well and we have the volume of engaged users to tell the right story."

Edwards is pleased with the work in progress.

"We're still trying to figure out our long-term strategy," she says. "Yes we can sell ads on our products, but can they be an acquisition channel, a new way we get volunteerism or donations? We're testing ideas."

AARP's advertisers have proceeded with a caution that Edwards says is not problematic.

By the fall of 2011 traffic to AARP's mobile website was 2 percent of its overall traffic, according to Edwards. But given the fact that there are 80 million visits a month, Edwards says the 2 percent "is not insignificant."

Have We Crossed the Chasm?

Michael Becker isn't a mobile lifer but he must feel that way. His first mobile exposure was in 1996, way before brands gave the channel a serious look.

"I break it down into eras," says Becker, the North America managing director for the Mobile Marketing Association (MMA). "2003 to
2007, brands were hardly involved in the conversation at all. It was all
about the technology and infrastructure, and to the extent that brands
were involved, it was technology-oriented companies. 2007 to 2009, it
was primarily the forward-looking companies and about experimentation. 2009 to 2010 was the broader R&D [research and development]
and experimentation discussion for a broader set of brands. 2010 to
2011, we saw the broader experimentation. Brands moved mobile from
the R&D budget to the mainline budget. 2011, we're seeing the next
tier of brand discussion where people are saying, 'I should get involved
in mobile. What should I do about it?' We're still in the crossing-the-
chasm stage. When you think about the brand being the early adopter,
we've just begun on the beachhead of the opposite site of the chasm,
if you will. We're in the very, very early stage of the majority of brand
adoption of mobile."

Becker continues:

"Once you get over the chasm, it moves pretty quickly and you go
up the adoption. The big issues are all about how quickly can we as an
industry start establishing benchmarks and getting better metrics and
educational tools out in the marketplace. The key is we've gone into
what the MMA calls recognition of the indispensible nature of mobile
in the marketing mix. More and more brands are recognizing the marketing imperative of having mobile.

"The question? 'Now that I know I have to do it, where do I start
and where do I go?' Part of the way I answer that is we've reached the
area of emotional intelligence of the necessity of mobile. We have not
yet reached the rational intelligence of mobile around execution and
delivery. We still have a ways to go there and what we need there is
additional evidence building from all the market verticals. We need to
get to the point of, 'OK, I get it. What does it mean to me?'"

I once copresented at an iMedia Connection conference with a
former Apple marketer who now runs digital strategy at an agency in
San Diego. As we collaborated on a presentation, she had only one
request—let's not present on what we believe will happen more than
six months from now.

"Of course, no one knows," she told me.

That's true, but it doesn't stop us from speculating.

Here's where Becker sees innovation taking us:

"Cloud-based services that leverage augmented reality. The AR [augmented reality] concept of how am I going to augment the screen for my experience is going to take traction in 2012 and into [20]13?

"Also, the recognition of pause and resume. That consumers will have an experience with a brand on one screen and that it moves and they expect that experience to move with them. With that pause and resume, consumers are going to want the best experience that [they] can have at a particular device at that particular time."

Becker envisions even more relevant experiences coming through mobile devices.

"I also see the importance of context growing more and more and beyond just location. Time will be the next access that will take a big role in our conversation. It's not just a matter that I'm in Times Square but when am I in it, because the engagement around you is different if I'm standing in Times Square at 12 in the afternoon versus 12 at night. How do we play that role and have that level of context with consumers?

"We're going to see the idea of permission marketing go beyond I got your opt in or opt out. There are going to be layers of permission. When can you talk to me? On what subjects? And on what devices and mediums?"

Sounds complicated? It may be for a time.

"I see a cube," Becker says. "We're going to a multidimensional managerial world of mobile where we have to manage ourselves around a cube rather than just a few parameters. This is going to be hard. If you think the axis of devices, traditional media types, mobile media types, and new media types like advertising and location permission management and privacy controls and market sectors and then by consumer experience and on incentive models such as couponing, retail stores, etc. It's the companies that can manage the dynamics within that cube for the needs of their business, and their consumers are going to be the ones that win."

Do We Have Enough Metrics to Make Wise Decisions?

As Frank Barbieri of YuMe and others have said, mobile has a ways to go before it can provide metrics that will provide more insight into performance. Some envision the day when mobile will be included in a so-called universal dashboard that provides a real-time view of all marketing programs regardless of channel.

It's a lofty goal and not one that necessarily will be met by a pure mobile company.

"We wrestled with this a bit internally and also on behalf of our customers," says Hipcricket chief operating officer Eric Harber. "Business intelligence, the BI field, has been around for a while. There are large companies that occupy that space. We're not going to be that company but we can play our part.

"We can provide a great centralized dashboard for mobile information. We can feed that into those incumbent [business intelligence] systems and have them give us the information we need in our system to retarget and re-serve with those learnings."

InsightExpress's Joy Liuzzo agrees that mobile campaigns should be viewed within the context of the larger marketing initiatives.

"For our clients, metrics were always important, even if they weren't ready to do mobile yet," she says. "Oftentimes the availability of metrics was what encouraged our clients to dip their toe into mobile. They knew they could compare mobile performance to their other media, providing executives with clear ROI [return on investment] and hopefully getting a larger budget for future campaigns.

"As the campaign budgets grew, we encouraged clients to expand their understanding by conducting cross-media studies to look at the synergistic impact of all their media, including mobile."

Microsoft's Barbara Williams, a former marketer at venerable Johnson & Johnson and Unilever, is working around the lack of precise mobile measurement.

"Now it seems to be very anecdotal," she says. "We know we spent x amount and we know the cost per engagement or cost per experience. We'll look at the percent we spend in media on mobile or media in other channels and look at the return on that in terms of visitors or engagement and try to compare it. We'll say we know we're not spending nearly as much in mobile as we are in digital but we're getting just as much traffic.

"Right now we're at the beginning stages of making it more scientific and more data driven. It is starting with that we need to collect the same data across all of our campaigns as a baseline and then whatever else goes on top of that specific to that campaign. Until we collect the data the same way, it is hard for us to make a data-driven decision and take action on that. That's where we're starting with the framework—understanding what we're measuring and making that consistent and standard across the company."

ESPN's John Kosner says that a bigger flow of brand dollars to mobile will solve the mobile metrics woes.

"It's weak now but in my experience the measurement follows the money," he says. "Everybody complains where it is now. I think we'll see significant expansion in the measurement in the next 5 to 10 years. In the meantime, I think companies like ours—that have great products, demonstrate scale, and represent a safe buy—we may benefit disproportionately in a world less measured.

"I think [the lack of strong metrics is] a frustration for marketers today but I think it's a mistake not to get started and learn this thing. Television has been an inefficient science forever and it is by far the most popular medium. This is going to be a booming business."

Will Consumers Continue to Seek Out Offers?

Duh.

Through more than 150,000 mobile campaigns, Hipcricket has found that mobile subscribers want a deal. That was true before, during, and after the recession. Since the beginning, brands have come to Hipcricket for simple delivery of deals—a text message sent in response to a call to action that can be shown at retail. In 2009 the company brought a more sophisticated solution to the market, providing single-use discount codes that consumers could key in anywhere a Visa or MasterCard was accepted.

The Yankee Group says that the number of active mobile coupon users is expected to grow from 2.7 million in 2010 to nearly 35 million in 2014.

If you are like me, you get frustrated when Groupon sends online offers for such nonsense as eyelash enhancement and flying trapeze lessons. The deals are sent to the masses rather than delivered in a highly personalized manner.

Actually, Groupon's most interesting offer to date doesn't involve a discount but instead a deal with consumers to provide relevant offers via its Groupon Now mobile service in exchange for user permission to factor in location and buying habit data.

In an e-mail to users, Groupon put it this way: "If you use a Groupon mobile app and you allow sharing through your device, Groupon may collect geo-location information from the device and use it for marketing deals to you."

Fortunately, Groupon spelled it out for us. In addition, Groupon stated in the e-mail that it might also collect other information (including relationship information, transaction information, financial account information, and mobile location information) and share it with Expedia, a travel company and Groupon partner.

No numbers have been given. Clearly some users have chosen to participate and others haven't and won't.

What's the Future of Mobile and Social?

As discussed previously, inserting the mobile device into the retail environment has changed the dynamic forever. Despite the hope of some businesses that the genie will get back in the bottle, don't expect it. Consumers have made information and access to their networks as important to their shopping experience as comfortable shoes.

I've yet to forget the Lexus salesman who in 2010 told me that I didn't know what I was talking about despite my access to invoice data available to me from *Consumer Reports* through my iPhone. Worse for him and the brand, even before leaving the dealership, I took to my social networks and spread word of my experience and displeasure.

Where are we headed?

The latest smartphones are capable of taking at least eight-megapixel photographs and capturing video in high definition. Graphic depictions of those *Moments of Trust* customer touch points are but an instant away from upload to Twitter, Facebook, and YouTube.

For marketers, those experiences can quickly impact brand perceptions and even sales. What are we to do about it? First, we need to plan to move quickly. Time is our enemy. Before we even get to the next negative experience, we need to impress on our organizations that customer service is more critical than ever. Further, we should celebrate successes at *Moments of Trust* and mitigate when a bad experience like the one with the Lexus salesman drags down our customer satisfaction scores.

Does My Vendor Protect Me?

Two guys in a garage may have the spiel down, but the question of whether their technology is their own is one that brand marketers should ask.

"You want your provider to have patents," says Hipcricket's chief technology officer Nathaniel Bradley. "Trade secrets that other companies utilize such as open source technologies are not adequate coverage. As you're selecting your vendor, one of the red flags would be an open source provider. Those open source providers are typically infringing on a United States patent holder that has the exclusive right to purvey particular aspects of technology services and products.

"Hipcricket has taken an investment and significant approach toward creating rights and defending rights within those patents. It speaks to quality of product. Patents are often signals of innovation. Patents ride on the very edge of innovation by their nature. They are required to be ahead of the market and it does indicate a foresight. Patents indemnify or protect the marketer by selecting a partner that is not going to yield litigations or other issues regarding the trampling upon other people's rights."

So just what should the patents cover?

"Mobile is particularly important with respect to device diversity," Bradley says. "There's a level to which the device and networks are extremely diverse with respect to their speed, to their operation and their capability. On a device itself, you have a browser, a platform, 3G, 4G connectivity rates, and devices that have particular software profiles. Different media players. It's analogous to the early Internet. You had dial-up users and broadband users and you had desktop users and Macintosh users.

"Hipcricket's patents stem from that time period where we invented technology that traversed those issues or solved that problem. There's a trade-off between content richness and audience. Marketers can't lose audience. So as they add content richness, they need a partner with adequate technology to traverse this spaghetti maze of all the product types and device types out there."

Of course, the carriers need to sign off on anything going across their networks.

"Our technology was developed to keep three constituents happy," Bradley says. "If you look at infrastructure providers, in particular with mobile, you never want to send down more information than you have to the device. You have limited processing capability, limited storage capacity—that's the nature of mobile. That obviously is being improved as next generations of smartphones come—it's becoming less and less an issue, just as it did with the Internet.

"In these early days of mobile marketing, it's particularly important to consider the infrastructure provider who wants to deliver a french fry rather than the whole potato. The end user who wants content relevant to themselves and wants to see content to them in particular in mobile advertising, there is geographic relevance, there are behavioral and other types of targeting that are ultimately beneficial to the consumer and keeping the consumer happy.

"Lastly, the content provider or the marketer wants to deliver the Ford F-150 ad as opposed to the Focus based on a particular profile. The marketers want to hit the consumers with information that they want, the consumers want the information that they want, and the infrastructure providers want to provide it in the most cost-effective and technically feasible way. Our invention reached across all three and provides for a tiny code module that scouts out the environment, scouts out the device, the software profile, the software plug-ins, and ultimately the consumer profile and delivers a tailored consumer response."

With permission granted, tailoring could include the recognition of such conditions as weather or time of day.

"If you look at the progression of that targeting, ambient targeting, which we also own a portfolio, has do with whether the sun was shining when you invoked a mobile marketing campaign, the last time you bought donuts it was raining, whether the stock market was up or down or whether your sales were up or down during a particular marketing campaign or mobile delivery," Bradley says. "All those ambient conditions contribute to a targeting that will become more and more enhanced. You can see in the future that if I picked up your cell phone by accident, it would be absolutely worthless to me because of the amount of targeting and the amount of customization of content that goes from device to device."

Will Transparency Move My Business?

As discussed, the shopping experience has changed forever. Some retailers have adapted and others have not.

"Transparency, whether you're intellectually honest with yourself or not, has massively increased," says Patrick Flanagan, vice president of digital strategy at Simon Property Group. "And whether you want to be an ostrich and stick your head in the sand and ignore it like, 'My price is what my price is and I don't care what someone else's price is.' For the short term, you'll probably get away with it. But there's a smarter way of saying how can we leverage it instead of being fearful of it and frustrated with it."

In-store, consumers are checking prices through mobile websites and apps, among other means. Flanagan sees a day where scanning becomes part of the regular shopping routine.

"Scanning doesn't have to mean buying online," he says. "It can be scan and check availability. Scan and check assortment. How about you scan and make wish lists? There are a lot of interesting use cases. The same behaviors will be done, but what happens after the scan, I think what's what will be interesting."

Brand marketer Rick Mathieson predicts monumental change at retail.

"We're going to see the beginnings of an evolution in what we call location-based services, and a convergence of several different trends that will radically redefine what we call mobile marketing and what we call retailing for the decade ahead," he says. "You'll see the convergence of things like Foursquare and Shopkick and so on, with things like the Layar augmented reality browser, with things like NFC [near field communication] and/or QR [quick response] codes— or whatever they evolve into—and retailers having their own apps that manage CRM [customer relationship management] systems and offer discounts. All of these things are going to converge in an interesting way.

"Here's how it will be manifest. You're Jane and you're walking into Hot Stuff Boutique. You're going to turn on the Hot Stuff app, and the store is instantly going to know Jane just walked in the door. You're going to instantly receive offers based on your stated preferences and your past purchase history. 'Hi Jane! If you loved those jeans you bought last month, you're going to love these new tops.' It'll even show you where the shirts are in the store. Should you decide to, you can send your information to the tablet device in the store clerk's hands, so he or she can give you very personalized customer care when you're in the store. When you walk over to the shirts, you'll be able to scan the tag to watch video of models wearing the shirts on the runway, or a video about the brand and the inspirations for the design."

There's more to Mathieson's scenario:

"When you go into the dressing room, you'll be able to capture video or images of yourself in the store mirror and instantly send it out to your social network for instant feedback on whether the style is 'fly' or 'forgettaboutit,'" he says. "If desired, you'll be able to grab accessories from the catalogue and superimpose them on your reflection using augmented reality and you in the store, and your friends out in the world, will be able to have a real-time shopping experience. Depending on what your friends say, or maybe despite what they say, if you decide you want that shirt, you might throw it in your bag or just wear it and walk right out of the store. New-fangled theft deterrent technology will be disabled, and the transaction will happen automatically and wirelessly, perhaps on the fly or with the tap of your phone on a NFC reader, because you've entered your credit card information into a Web portal associated with the app or because you have mobile wallet capabilities. And you're on your way—without digging for cash, writing a check, swiping a card or ever again standing in line.

"At every point of communications—advertising or retail—you will be able to take action through the mobile device in unprecedented ways. It will be your remote control for the entire world."

We may even see e-tailer Amazon set up brick-and-mortar stores.

"Amazon has carved out a nice market for itself that will continue to grow in the coming days," says wireless analyst Chetan Sharma. "In some sense, with its tight integration of commerce, cloud, and advertising, it has outmaneuvered even Google.

"Amazon's impact will be felt by many others in 2012 as its strategy becomes more apparent. Retailers will be facing the brunt of the wave that Amazon represents (i.e., e-tailers supplanting physical retailers). Don't be surprised if Amazon pursues Apple-like stores to showcase its merchandise and puts a dagger at the heart of retail."

How Will Mobile Change with the Passing of Steve Jobs?

Much like I remember where I was when I learned the tragic news that John Lennon had been shot (I was watching *Monday Night Football* and heard it from broadcaster Howard Cosell), I'll now never forget where I was and what I was doing when I learned of Steve Jobs's passing on October 5, 2011.

It's rather fitting that I was 36,000 feet in the air connected to an in-flight Wi-Fi system working on a MacBook Air at the time. Thus, I was able to benefit from the technology advancements made possible by visionaries like Jobs who have brought us all advantages that generations before us would never know.

And that brings me to another connection between Lennon and Jobs. Each asked us to imagine and look beyond the here and now to what will be—if we are open to it.

In this respect, the contributions by Lennon and Jobs are tied to imagination and what can happen when we free our minds. They reshaped our thinking about peace, technology, and the world around us. And through their vision and passion they made our world a better place.

To me, this is their legacy and the biggest lesson they have taught us. Dare to dream. Strive to have impact. Rather than accept limitations that would normally convince us that we can't do something, these two men—in their own fiercely individual ways—showed us that with hard work and dedication we can do anything we put our minds to.

Jobs's biggest influence on mobile marketing and advertising is in the way the iPhone and iPad changed behavior.

Never before had we had such pleasing user experiences and access to content on our terms via the real Web and the revolutionary App Store.

For years, literally, I've been waiting for a Web page to load properly on my BlackBerry.

Jobs's contributions in those areas will be remembered more fondly than Apple's early mobile advertising efforts called iAd that were billed as "Advertising Reimagined."

iAd will go down as a milestone because of the reported $300 million that Apple paid for Quattro Wireless in 2010 to build out the iAd network. That move followed Google's outmaneuvering of Apple for the 2009 purchase of mobile ad firm AdMob late in 2009.

As one might expect, iAd was introduced by Jobs as revolution-ary. In typical Jobsesque-fashion, he called out the mobile industry for what Jobs said were low-quality ad executions.

"Well, we've got a lot of free apps—we like that, users like that, but these developers have to find a way to make some money, and we'd like to help them," he said in 2010. "What some of them are starting to do is put mobile ads in their apps and most of this advertising sucks. We want to help developers make money with ads so they can keep their free apps free.

"On a mobile device, search is not where it's at, not like on the desktop. They're spending all their time on these apps—they're using apps to get to data on the Internet, not generalized search. The average user spends over 30 minutes using apps on their phone. If we said we wanted to put an ad up every three minutes, that'd be 10 ads per device per day—about the same as a TV show. We're going to soon have 100 million devices. That's a billion ad opportunities per day."

Jobs's sell continued.

"This is a pretty serious opportunity, and it's an incredible demo-graphic," he said. "But we want to do more than that. We want to change the quality of the advertising."

As is Apple's way, Jobs always wanted to recreate the system. He commanded a minimum of $1 million from charter advertisers, including AT&T, Target, Turner Broadcasting System, Unilever, and Disney, and offered them only ads running on devices running Apple's operating system iOS. Million-dollar mobile buys were uncommon in those days, and the first brands were buying buzz as much as consumer interaction.

By many accounts, the early iAd programs were less than Apple-type home runs.

But although iAd has been short on return for brands and Apple ultimately greatly lowered its minimums, the company's dollars and efforts have validated the mobile advertising business models pursued by many others.

Meanwhile, the impact of Jobs's passing on Apple and on mobile in general will play out over several years at least.

"If there's anything I'm envious about Steve Jobs, it was his ability to see the vision, to continue to drive what was not possible and make it possible," says Hipcricket's Ivan Braiker. "To me, that's a lot of fun and intriguing. I feel very honored and lucky to be in a business that is moving as fast as it is—that you get to see the changes happening as fast as they happen."

Should We Be Looking for Innovation or the Maturing of Existing Technology?

As to what's next, Barbara Williams of Microsoft and Jonathan Dunn of Bell Media in Canada see more maturing of technologies than the introduction of something new that will dramatically change mobile marketing and advertising.

"Innovation will come through mobile commerce and the use of mobile devices in shopping decisions," Williams says. "I think it's the idea of driving commerce whether it's through the device or the device leading to the store to drive commerce also using the other technologies to enable that whether it's augmented reality, SMS [short message service], or different forms of geo-targeting. Gaming, social. Using all the different types of mobile technologies and integrating them in a meaningful way that will drive sales or commerce or drive people down the funnel.

"I don't know if innovation comes in new technology or combining what we have already in meaningful ways. People were throwing things against the wall. But when you think about it more strategically and think about the customer journey and that funnel or whatever shape you want to give it, you're going to start combining things in different ways that ultimately will create something new but components of it are known and exist today."

Dunn is looking for adoption of mobile technologies as the next big thing.

"In the mobile media and advertising space, in the next 12 to 18 months I see broader update and consolidation of existing innovations," he says. "We'll see the widespread build out of HTML5 websites/web apps, and tablet sites. We'll see mobile-rich media ad units becoming commonplace. At the same time, I'm optimistic we'll define best practices for each to ensure good user experiences that maintain the vitality of mobile media and respect the personal nature of the mobile device. I also expect significant improvements in ad targeting and analytics. Both will get more precise and flexible, which will increase their potency.

"Broadly, I think NFC [near field communication] is a huge opportunity for marketers. Payment and mobile wallet gets a lot of ink currently and while that's important, I think the real play will be in loyalty. The ability to personalize a customer experience and tie that into device features and user data is powerful. If rumors prove accurate, Apple is including NFC in a next version of the iPhone, which will be a watershed moment. Google is pushing the envelope, but Apple has an excellent track record in frictionless UX as well as a distribution and payment platform that's deeply integrated into peoples' lives. As always, privacy controls will be a huge topic."

Dunn is less sure about other topics.

"Less clear to me is how solutions like augmented reality (AR) and QR [quick response] codes will fare," he says. "I'm bullish on image recognition generally, but I have a harder time envisioning a widespread use of AR and QR that is elegant and sustainable in a way that isn't disruptive to how people actually use technology. Google's Goggles product has validated the concept of visual search, but it seems to me there's a much richer vein of activity when you can tie image recognition to other attributes like location awareness and the social/communication capabilities."

In Latin America, large change will likely be driven by the mobile operators.

"I expect the innovation in [Latin America] will come from the carriers' side, as I expect more creative models to increase user adoption of new tools and services," says Terence Reis, director of operations/partner at pontomobi interactive and a former Mobile Marketing Association managing director. "As far as we're talking about technical innovation, we're unfortunately still tied to a copycat attitude, looking at the United States and E.U. [European Union] and trying to copy whatever we think will be successful in the tropics.

"But if we're talking global, I see one big trend—which is the convergence between 'standard Internet' and mobile, turning everything into one streamlined flow of content, powered by the cloud. Our challenge will be how to create a story that's coherent among many devices and screens. And sensors. Everywhere. Not in the next 18 months, though. But the smartphones and feature phones will be senseless at some point, and we'll find out that we don't have a mobile or a phone or whatever in our hands. We have a PID—sorry for the awkward acronym. A personal identification device."

How Do I Find a Job in Mobile?

There is a constant amid the uncertainty in a mobile industry with so much dramatic change that it often feels like it's on steroids.

Employers from agencies to brands to vendors can't fill the jobs fast enough.

"Getting into mobile was the best thing I ever did," says Doug Stovall, Hipcricket senior vice president of sales and client services. "I was lucky to be in the right place at the right time. I certainly wasn't out there saying I'm going to be a mobile guy. I was just a technology guy working at a systems integrator. But it was the best thing to happen to me. I had a great run—it continues to be a great run."

Stovall is among those in search of more runners.

"I'm looking for people smarter than me," he says. "That's not very hard. It's hard to find good people in mobile. There are a lot of people with mobile experience—it doesn't necessarily mean that they're good. Candidly I can look at a lot of our competitors [and see] guys who are considered thought leaders and say that they are not smart people. I don't think they know a lot of mobile and I think they blow a lot of hot air.

"That's one thing that makes Hipcricket great. We have a lot of smart, professional people. When I go out and hire people, I look for people who can be as smart as they can be and who can work with integrity that puts the customer first. They need to believe in the things that we stand for, which is a 'can do' attitude, and doing what's right for the customer. If you want to do that, giddy up."

One avenue to the marketers eying a position in mobile is through the Mobile Marketing Association's certification program that I cocreated with Michael Becker, who is now the MMA's North America managing director. The Tier 1 certification exam covers topics, including fundamentals of mobile marketing, key industry terminology, regulatory requirements for mobile campaigns, consumer best practices, codes of conduct, budgetary and financial planning for mobile campaigns, and advanced knowledge of industry resources.

The exam consists of 50 multiple-choice questions and candidates have one hour to complete the test. One must achieve a minimum mark of 88 percent to become an MMA-certified mobile marketer.

Certification is open to marketers, product managers, QA (quality assurance) testers, account managers, and other mobile professionals involved in mobile campaigns, with all levels of expertise in mobile marketing.

Another path for would-be mobile marketers is through universities and colleges, including Ball State University in Muncie, Indiana, that has an extensive Emerging Media program with what it calls immersive learning.

"Mobile is just going to continue to explode," Stovall says. "What you'll see, I'm not sure how quickly this will occur, maybe 10 or 15 years, that you stop talking about it in terms of mobile. Desktop. iPad. It's just all one thing. You can start seeing the lines blur already. I thought that we would get away from calling things mobile or wireless. I thought there would be some other kind of word like when automobiles were invented, they were the horseless carriage. But then the name automobile came. Mobile is the same way. I don't know what mobile is—is an iPad mobile?"

Perhaps. But those of us in the industry are moving too fast to stop and consider name changes.

I often tell job applicants that the ones who thrive in mobile are those who can adapt and even embrace dizzying change.

"You have to have the stomach for it," says Hipcricket CFO Tom Virgin.

How Do I Select a Mobile Marketing Provider?

As I trust this book has shown, mobile marketing has proved to be one of the best ways not only to reach customers and prospects but to also engage them, thereby increasing sales and customer loyalty. However, many brands don't know where to begin.

For me, the first step is selecting the best provider for you, and, afterward, getting the most out of the relationship.

When selecting a firm, some areas of probing are obvious and involve traditional agency-client queries such as chemistry and bandwidth. But given mobile's relative nascency, others issues are more subtle yet just as important. Here are some questions to get started:

Question: Is the vendor a member of the Mobile Marketing Association (MMA) or does it at least abide by MMA guidelines?

Why it matters: Beyond the important area of best practices, a mobile marketing firm should keep you out of trouble, steering you clear of blunders like buying and marketing to a list, and creating content that might mistakenly be viewed by children. The MMA guidelines, created in part by member companies, are written to help brands avoid such transgressions.

Question: Does the provider have extensive carrier connections and relationships?

Why it matters: Connectivity to all the mobile operators gives you the assurance that all your customers and prospects can take part in your program. Solid relationships between your vendor and the carriers often move proposed campaigns along faster.

Question: Will the vendor be strategic and creative or purely on the execution side?

Why it matters: You have business goals, and your mobile dollars need to help you achieve them. It's important to align your brand with thinkers and innovators rather than pure workhorses.

Question: Will this partner help me build or expand my customer marketing database?

Why it matters: Beyond just a marketing tactic, mobile is a tool to help you create, manage, and monetize permission-based, opt-in databases.

Question: Is the vendor a mobile expert or new to the party?

Why it matters: If the agency was a search engine optimization expert last Thursday and now hangs a mobile sign on its door, how much help can you count on its expertise?

Question: Does the provider have solid references and ongoing relationships (as opposed to a history of one-off promotions)?

Why it matters: Given its permission-based nature, mobile marketing lends itself to sustained programs. Ask for references from clients on annual contracts that are leveraging dollars spent for ongoing engagement and success.

Question: If you want to use text as a component of your program, will they provide a dedicated short code and its inherent advantages?

Why it matters: If you are a pizza company doing mobile on a shared short code, the keyword *Pizza* is likely taken. Plus, having a dedicated short code is an imperative aspect of building your unique database, which can be a vital part of your customer relationship management program.

Question: Will your business goals be met if you choose a vendor purely on price?

Why it matters: Although mobile might be new to you, it's like everything else—you get what you pay for.

Question: Are there tools you can access, allowing you to view your campaign in real time and make adjustments along the way?

Why it matters: Optimization often makes or breaks mobile campaigns—insist on the ability to look at how your program is performing in real time so you can make changes if necessary. For example, we've seen clients extend street team activities and also recut broadcast spots in order to deliver the results they were expecting.

Question: Does the vendor have the capabilities you need to deliver your unique brand experience?

Why it matters: The first rule in branding is consistency across touch points. Mobile has a unique set of challenges, including the need to produce marketing materials to be viewed on hundreds of handsets with varying levels of sophistication. The agencies that can produce consistent brand experiences across devices are the keepers.

Question: Can the provider handle peaks in message volume, perhaps around a live event?

Why it matters: It's all about the user experience. For example, if your intent is to offer a free burger to concert goers as they leave an arena, it's critical to reach the consumer in a timely way.

Question: Is there a record of return on investment (ROI), especially in your category?

Why it matters: Some industries—automotive and quick-service restaurants, for example—produce better results on mobile than other categories. Just as in traditional marketing, there are nuances that can make or break campaigns. Agencies with repositories of case studies can show you what works and what doesn't.

Mobile isn't especially complicated, but tapping into the correct agency's expertise will move you faster from strategy to development to results.

Twitter vs. Mobile: How to Decide?

With time and budget being so precious, marketers considering using Twitter and/or mobile marketing must ask important questions: Are they interchangeable, complementary, or even necessary?

In the case of Twitter, with a strategic and concerted effort, a brand can reach large numbers of customers and prospects. Many have found Twitter to be a means to create buzz. But there are thousands of applications that enhance the Twitter experience. It's not enough to just understand Twitter—a marketer must also know which application to use and when.

In the world of mobile marketing, text messaging is an impressive phenomenon. But how does a brand create a dialogue via text that is permission-based and of value?

Back to Twitter—the successes are impressive.

Just look at Dell, which has shown Twitter to be a revenue driver. In a case study posted on Twitter's website, the computer manufacturer says it has booked more than $3 million in revenue through 80 Dell-branded Twitter accounts.

On the same site, JetBlue says its Twitter initiatives are breaking down "artificial walls" between consumers and the airline.

Still, many other brands have yet to be converted. Their hesitancies range from concerns around the lack of standardized measurement (is it the number of followers, the quality of followers, or what is being said and by whom?) to questions about how to make noise in such a noisy environment, as well as how to have a one-to-one relationship in such a public forum.

These same concerns don't apply on the mobile marketing side of things, where successful campaigns often employ programs to give marketers the one-to-one relationship they seek. Through permission-based programs, brands are then able to seize on the opportunity created when a consumer responds first to an offer, then says yes to the follow-up asking whether he or she wants to opt in to a mobile club for additional offers and information.

Other advantages of opt-in mobile programs over Twitter include the following:

- Guarantee of reaching consumers on their mobile phones. Although some Twitter users receive updates on their mobile phones, there is no way to know exactly how many actually do.
- Greater audience size. Would a business advertise on only one radio station? One TV station? One billboard? Twitter has more than 100 million members, according to the company, but many are inactive. By contrast, according to CTIA–The Wireless Association, more than 200 million Americans text message on a regular basis.
- Legitimate text-based contests, polls, and mobile coupon campaigns. There is no seamless way to do this on Twitter.
- Established guidelines as developed by the carriers and Mobile Marketing Association; with Twitter, there are only rules of thumb.
- Multiple-step campaigns that allow a business to generate warm, opted-in leads.
- Ease of integration with traditional advertising to effectively measure and compute ROI. Twitter cannot be combined with traditional advertising in a meaningful, effective manner, nor can it provide reports and charts.

Of course, Twitter has made a difference for hundreds if not thousands of brand marketers and subsequently is a medium that all practitioners must keep their eyes on. In fact, if you visit Twitter.com you will see that Twitter lists the following best practices for marketers looking to leverage the service.

Key points include:

- Keep a tally of questions answered, customer problems resolved, and positive exchanges held on Twitter. Do the percentages change over time?

- When you offer deals via Twitter, use a unique coupon code so that you can tell how many people take you up on that Twitter-based promotion. If you have an online presence, you can also set up a landing page for a promotion to track not only click-throughs but further behavior and conversations.
- Use third-party tools to figure out how much traffic your websites are receiving from Twitter.
- Track click-throughs on any link you post in a tweet.

Obviously, today's marketers will need to stay current to tap into ever-changing consumer behaviors and interests. The opportunities are great, but so are potential pitfalls.

Can I Capitalize on the Hyperlocal Opportunity?

A growing number of businesses are sharpening their focus on hyperlocal advertising and marketing. Still in its nascent stage, hyperlocal presents an attractive opportunity: the power to engage with customers at the optimum time and place.

The catalysts behind the hyperlocal trend fall into two camps. First is the continued maturation of technologies, namely those capable of delivering marketers the information they need to determine a consumer's precise location.

Today there are multiple categories of information that businesses can tap into, including derived information (mobile phone number, area code, etc.); declared information (registration process, hotel check-ins, VIP clubs); network-initiated information (triangulation, carrier, Wi-Fi, hot spot); and GPS (iPhone, Android, BlackBerry, Symbian, Windows Mobile).

The second driving force behind the hyperlocal trend is the fact that consumers have voiced an interest in locally driven communications. In fact, according to the MMA, half of mobile users who noticed any ads while using location-based services took action. The MMA also found that most mobile users are "interested in allowing their phone to automatically share their location in exchange for perks, such as free use of mobile applications and mobile coupons." These are meaningful numbers that clearly demonstrate why a growing number of brands are looking to latch on to this trend.

With these figures in mind, the temptation to jump into the hyperlocal waters is high. However, before taking action, marketers are advised to first run through the following quick hyperlocal marketing checklist:

- Determine whether your business has a large enough customer base to warrant such an investment. Hyperlocal is best suited for businesses trying to move products that have value but also a limited shelf life. A good example would be a flower chain looking to unload the remainder of their summer flowers for a nice discount or a Starbucks franchise looking to sell off its remaining stock of Pumpkin Spice Lattes before the Eggnog Latte season kicks off. Businesses also must have real-time, 24/7 visibility into inventory and the ability to see what is available at any given moment.
- Conducting frequent competitor assessments is a classic business exercise that remains essential. Look at what your competitors are doing. Have they already deployed a hyperlocal campaign? If so, chances are they are grabbing your customers right now. For example, if coffee chain A is offering 50 percent off a latte to local area customers, why wouldn't they break their commitment to coffee chain B? This is especially important if your product can be viewed as somewhat of a commodity. If your competitors are already there, you need to move now. If they have not taken action, you have an opportunity to be the first to the punch.
- Consumer trust is critical to the success of any business and nowhere is a potential violation of this confidence more precarious than with a hyperlocal campaign. The most common perception is that this type of campaign consists of businesses firing off marketing offers to a consumer's mobile device willy-nilly whenever they pass a store. In fact, many industry pundits believe that hyperlocal won't arrive until that model hits the mainstream.

However, the truth is quite the opposite. Consumers don't want to be inundated by brands every time they pass their local Starbucks. Your customers are interested in receiving locally relevant ads on their terms. Hyperlocal is about creating a community experience for the consumer that's relevant to their area, whether it's where they work or live, or both. Within this community, brands should develop an intelligent hyperlocal campaign that has a cadence, delivering relevant messages to consumers perhaps twice a month rather than every few hours.

Although attracting new customers is essential for the livelihood of any business, the hyperlocal effort is really best suited for your current customer roster. If you're ultimately looking to strengthen your customer's commitment to your brand, then hyperlocal is for you. Approach these customers with the opportunity to opt in to your hyperlocal community. For those who reciprocate, you then have the opportunity to present them with attractive offers on a consistent albeit infrequent basis. In doing so, businesses will be able to cultivate more frequent repeat visits. There's no price tag you can put on that.

As the focus on local continues to grow, more businesses will be faced with the hyperlocal question. Examining the details above should help these businesses determine whether it's the right path for them.

35

Advice from the Smartest Marketers

THE BEST PART ABOUT writing this book is the opportunity I have been given to talk to—and learn from—some of the brightest and innovative marketing minds working around the world. Each eagerly passed along their insights, hoping like I do that the readers of *Mobilized Marketing*, not to mention me, will become better equipped to gauge, use, and succeed with mobile.

Always generous, Hank Wasiak, a communications industry leader who has worked with the corporate elite of global business throughout his 40-year career, generously shared his views on how best to meet the consumer.

"Technology opened the door to what consumers always felt anyway—back in my day when we were doing IR [infrared] scores to gauge television commercials and saying how hard it was to break through, the average recall for a 30-second spot was maybe 25 percent of the people who were forced to look at a commercial would remember it," he says. "They were telling us then, 'I want it the way I want it when I want it.' We just didn't have the capability to do it. Now we do.

Mobile, it gets you connected but it's part of your life in a functional way, in an emotional way, an entertaining way, in a lifesaving way."

And Wasiak, the former vice chairman of McCann Erickson WorldGroup, says fire sooner rather than later.

"To me, the key thing when looking at something is to be early and fast," he says. "I've been the poster child for this. You want to over-think things sometimes. You want to get it perfect but things move so fast. To me in this world, especially in mobile, iteration is more important than innovation. You can find out quickly because you're in real time in the hip pocket, the breast pocket and in the heart of your consumers.

"You have to put on a flak jacket and get a little more risk averse."

These days Wasiak teaches University of Southern California undergraduate and graduate students nearly 50 years his junior. Actually, as he freely admits, they teach him.

"No offense to my grad school students but I learn a lot more from the undergraduates about social and mobile," he says. "They are much more free with it, they're much more involved with it. There is no—zero—tolerance for bullshit. They are very respectful for the responsibility of transparency [in marketing].

"It encourages the hell out of me."

Get Mobile to Go Mobile

Microsoft's Barbara Williams has easy-to-follow instructions for those in search of more learning.

"This is something really simple," she says. "If you're not sure if you should be doing mobile, take a page out of classic consumer research model and do ethnographic research. You can do it on your own. Go to the store, go to the mall, go out to dinner, and sit back and watch people. Just watch. Old school. And you see everyone is on their devices and they are spending quite a bit of time on their devices and they're not making phone calls necessarily and they are not just doing SMS [short message service]—they are doing a lot of things.

"When you see that happening around you everywhere you go, think about how can I insert my product or my brand or my message into these experiences. Just look at the world around you. And listen to young people who grew up in the digital age. Their behaviors are completely different. You'll see this is definitely the route to go in. Invest the time to learn it and understand it. Explore it yourself."

Hipcricket founder Ivan Braiker also believes in the power of observation.

"What marketers do and should do is look around," he says. "It doesn't take much more than that. I don't know anybody in this country from the teens on up that is ever any farther away than three feet from their mobile phone. It's the way that everybody engages today.

"Look at time that people spend around that mobile phone versus any other media. Look at the ability to do what a marketer always considered nirvana or the Holy Grail—have that one-on-one relationship. From folks from Seth Godin on down who want to talk about building community and tribes, I would challenge anybody to tell me a better way to do it. I know marketers are always hesitant and would rather follow than lead, but I think at this time there are enough proven capabilities with huge ROIs [returns on investment] based around mobile. The ROIs alone should dictate that mobile should be part of what they're doing and in their marketing goals."

Alter Course or Have Thick Skin

Asked what he would say to a marketer who has yet to explore the use of mobile marketing, Terence Reis offers three alternatives:

"'Dude, you're stupid or what?

"I think I saw you in that movie *Jurassic Park*.

"You're losing an opportunity to start a unique conversation with your customers. You'll find customers on mobile will start a conversation only if they trust you and they expect transparency and good services. You'll be forced to learn how to talk to people again. And your company will find that it's not only a matter of talking—the negative points of your products will be thrown mercilessly at your inbox. But if you have the guts you'll be in control and will have the chance to improve your product and your relationship with your audience.

"Oh, this is important. You don't have only consumers anymore. You'll have an audience. Big difference in terms of behavior. As the standard measure of success for an audience is attention."

Be on the Lookout for the Wave

Michael Bayle stops short of pinning a stupidity tag on those who haven't tried mobile. On the other hand, he doesn't call them savvy, either.

"These are the same kind of marketers who didn't appreciate what search was going to become and look where they are now," says the ESPN executive. "And similarly they didn't appreciate the revolution of social media advertising that Facebook has pioneered. Where are they now?

"They have two choices—they can either ride the wave or watch the wave pour over them. We can equip them with a surfboard, equip them with the right tools so that it's just not an investment and a spend but there's tactically at the end of the day some return on investment we're collectively monitoring that is better for their brand."

Bayle says consumers have new and high expectations when it comes to mobile interactions.

"At the end of the day, it's not that their fans aren't expecting to see their brands on mobile," he says. "In fact, if anything, they are questioning, 'How come I'm not seeing this brand interact with me on this set of mediums because I see them all the time on television and print, why don't they have a mobile site?'

"I would remind them that their own consumers, and in our case, the fans, have an expectation to have a mobile site, not unlike what you saw between 1995 and 2000, which was a gradual, then rapid expansion of every major brand and every major marketer finally putting up their dot-com sites slowly but surely and ultimately appreciating the benefits and return on investment. The same thing is now happening with mobile."

Hipcricket chief operating officer Eric Harber's advice is to think first about desired business results.

"Mobile is finally taking off in earnest, period," he says. "There is no debate. It's got to be return on investment. It can no longer be a fad. This is not just because it's cool and everyone is doing a mobile app because there's a reason to spend those dollars in that channel.

"If you haven't started mobile, then you are playing catch-up. The most important thing to keep in mind is that it has got to be pragmatic. There's a place for experimentation, trying something cool, throwing something against the wall and see if it sticks. We certainly enable our customers to do this. We also counsel our customers because we are their trusted strategic partner that build the house, if you will, on a strong foundation. It's important to get high-quality help. It can save you time and money."

Canadian marketer Jonathan Dunn throws in the idea of testing.

"Mobile is growing and won't be slowing down in the foreseeable future," he says. "More people are getting smartphones and those that have them are spending more time with them. If mobile is still on the low part of its inevitable growth curve, isn't now the time to understand how to effectively activate your brand in mobile? Take the time to test and learn now. You can define your own best practices and use cases so that when mobile is at a scale that demands a much larger share of the budget, you can maximize your ROI.

"The size of the audience may vary but the simple 'what does your brand site look like on a mobile phone and is that the type of experience you want to offer customers' test' can be hugely compelling. No marketer who values himself or herself as a brand advocate or guardian will be satisfied with a nonmobile-optimized experience. The reality is that consumers are looking to engage brands on mobile and are increasingly intolerant of poor experiences. Most consumers probably don't understand the finer points of mobile development, [operating system] fragmentation, or device detection. They just want something that works and makes it easy to get what they want."

Dunn is careful to not call marketers in his home country stupid.

"From a purely Canadian point of view, I'd be understanding of a company that has not embraced mobile, as mobile in Canada has been hurt by a lack of research on Canadians' mobile behavior. We could use U.S. data but that's directional at best. To make investments in new channels, we needed to produce homegrown data. The good news is, that's changing and the research obstacle won't be valid for much longer, if it still is at all."

Don't Offer Excuses

Marketers never have enough time in their days. That isn't going to change.

What Hipcricket's Doug Stovall says should change is mobile's place on the list of priorities.

"I just think that it's a crock if they can't figure out an opportunity," says Stovall, Hipcricket's senior vice president of sales and client services. "There are so many opportunities. What it comes down to is they may not have the time. There's always budget. Marketers can always find budget. Mobile is inexpensive.

"My thing to any marketer is to get in the game. Spend some money on mobile and, at a minimum, buy mobile advertising. There are a million companies that will talk to you. What I would say is don't talk to two guys in a garage. Find a real company that has done a lot of campaigns. Bring them in and let them make you smart."

That includes broadcast stations still finding their way when it comes to new media, including mobile.

"I think you have to do mobile, but I just don't know that it's the savior that people think," he says. "People here at Hipcricket said we're going to take mobile and it's going to be the savior for radio. Guess what? Mobile is phenomenal but mobile needs to be one seat in the overall marketing channel. It's not going to cure AIDS. It's not going to fix the hunger problem in Africa. What it can do is it can add value to traditional media. We have seen that it helps make TV somewhat measurable. We can see in radio that it helps radio generate revenue. But unless you really work mobile, it doesn't save the day."

Watch for Small and Large Changes

Mario Schulzke, founder of IdeaMensch and director of digital strategy at marketing firm WDCW, is one of those Gen-Xers who teaches Boomers like me something every day. His insights for us are to keep an eye on the little guy as well as the titans.

"You know, I am not smart enough to tell you about major game changers," Schulzke says. "But I can tell you there will be a revolution of incremental innovations that are about to take place. It's so easy nowadays to build your own website, your own piece of software or your own app. So what's happening is that a bunch of people are starting to solve the problems that they've been having in their own lives and industries. We'll see some major productivity gains in just about every vertical, driven by people solving problems close to their vest."

Sure, there's a learning curve in mobile. Schulzke says much of the path comes by following one's instincts.

"Do what feels right," he says. "Build a marketing program around tactics that make sense for you. I have many clients who are overwhelmed by Twitter, Facebook, Foursquare, and the like. But when we talk about creating content that provides value to existing and potential customers, they get that. Having a roundtable discussion on Twitter is no different than going to a networking meeting. Crafting a webinar and capturing leads via e-mail is no different than speaking at your local Lion's Club.

"Do what makes sense to you, and always think about the value you provide to your audience. Focus on the fundamentals. Respectfully communicate with your customers via all channels. Don't pretend to be something you're not, and do the right thing."

Look Beyond the Obvious

With wireless facilitating quick and easy transmission and receipt of information, pictures, and other content, Mary Furlong advises marketers to think broader than their core target audience.

"What people are not getting are the drivers for the change in behavior with the younger generation communicating with the older generation," says Furlong, an expert on marketing to Boomers. "For example, a young woman could be expecting her first baby and so she's in the Kate Spade store to choose which diaper bag to get. She sends her mom a picture of the diaper bag and the mom's going to say let me get that for you. Kate Spade would never be thinking that the market is an older market but in fact it very much is."

Think Beyond the Funnel

For more than a century, marketers have talked about a customer journey that they hope will lead to the purchase of a product or service. Called the purchasing funnel, the process goes from awareness to action.

Mobile may have changed a 100-year-old process.

"It's not a funnel anymore," says Microsoft's Barbara Williams. "It's becoming a different kind of shape. We know that you're driving loyalty with mobile social but you are also driving awareness and going back to the top of the funnel. The key for great marketing, and it's more imperative for mobile, is to look at the entire journey and understand the role that mobile can play to continue that journey and continue the path for that person back up [the funnel] again—and to strengthen and connect mobile with other parts of your digital campaign and other parts of your traditional campaign.

"You have to look holistically, then you have to look specifically within mobile and that's part of the reason why it's so complex, because you have to think in different ways."

Remember Mobile Is Not the Same as Online

Among the differences Microsoft's Williams cites in comparing online and mobile is in the area of rich media.

"When you think rich media and digital, you tend to think of the standbys like a whole page takeover or part of an ad will be in the leaderboard at the top of the page and move into one of the units on the side," she says. "On mobile, it's a completely different type of experience. You don't have the flexibility but you have the entire device. You can incorporate rich functionality where you can shake the device or where it is actually using the camera function in augmented reality or the location function. There are so many other vectors or parameters that are unique to mobile that I think make rich even richer on mobile. But you have to think about it in a different way on mobile.

"Depending on who you talk to in the ecosystem, if you talk to folks who are either media vendors or media buyers or planners, we can have rich media that could include all the content and engagement that you want in the ad itself, which is true but if you design it really well, it's not possible to cover all the scenarios that your user might want to learn about. If it's done its job, they will want to go further. If you don't have a mobile landing page attached to that rich media unit, you have kinda left them hanging. While rich media is an incredible opportunity to pull people in and to really drive engagement and surface up and push the content out, that back end is still needed when they want to continue their journey if it's done its job really well."

Find Multiple Ways to Engage

In tune with her audience, Eileen Woodbury, director of marketing at Clear Channel Los Angeles, has made choice the centerpiece of her marketing initiatives.

"People will communicate with you the way they want to communicate," she says. "So texting isn't replacing the Web. The Web didn't replace the phone call. People who want to call will want to call. People who never called us before hopefully will engage with us through text. Some people prefer Twitter or are on Facebook all day.

"This is the age of choice. People communicate the way they want to. With every new thing that comes along, we're adding to our arsenal."

Surprisingly many of Woodbury's counterparts are still on the sidelines, and she can't figure out why.

"It frustrates me but, at the same time, you guys [Hipcricket employees] say we do a good job with it . . . I still think that we don't," she says. "I feel sometimes we can get lazy with it and [are] still not using it to its full extent.

"If you're telling me people don't use it to the extent we do, it is shocking to me. More than frustrating, I find it shocking."

Think One to One, Not One to Many

All these years into mobile and we still get asked about the cost of acquiring a list. These questions obviously come from those who haven't done just the tiniest bit of homework to see that mobile is purely permission-based and that the mobile operators will quickly shut you down if you spam rather than build your own opt-in database.

The second most asked database question is about size. How many opted-in consumers does one need to make it meaningful?

"A lot of people at radio stations and brands think that you have to start with this big database," says Gay Gabrilska, a former Hipcricket client who is now the company's vice president of mobile solutions. "They ask, 'Where do I buy this database?' not understanding that it's a little more grassroots, a little more tribal.

"It is kind of along the lines of social media now. If you had the right message, you could really drive those numbers."

Reconsider Traditional Media

One of radio's biggest champions is Clear Channel's Kris Foley, who disagrees with those who say that the medium's heyday is behind us. "Mobile has taken radio, which is considered a traditional media, and put a very sexy face on it," she says. "It has modernized us in many ways. People are very excited about having mobile in their campaigns. One-stop shopping makes us different—the only way you'll have integrated stations is if you have online, on air, and mobile working together. We'll see more clients adapt to text."

Conclusion

So Where Are We with Mobile Marketing?

LIKE MANY, LOUIS GUMP entered the mobile world by circumstance. He was doing online business development for the Weather Channel in 2001 when his company identified a match between a consumer with a mobile device and a weather product that was needed every day.

Over the next decade, he was arguably mobile's biggest champion, traveling worldwide to evangelize on behalf of the Weather Channel, CNN, and the Mobile Marketing Association.

"I believed from about day two of what was happening in mobile that this was going to be a very big deal," he says. "I'm not at all surprised. However, I'll say that there was a lot of uncertainty. But the phone is turning into the new generation of a personal computer in the literal sense of both words. Actually I think in some ways we've just come light years and in other ways we're just beginning. I'm not at all surprised but I'm so pleased to see it happening because I felt like the indications were there. But I also don't think that it was inevitable.

"A lot of this couldn't have gone this way. What if we didn't have the iPhone today? Imagine a world without the iPhone. What if the carriers hadn't implemented cross-carrier text messaging and picture interchange? What if we didn't have 4G today? What if we didn't have advertisers who see this as a very effective channel? There are a lot of things that didn't have to go well."

Gump says the doubters can't see the forest from the trees.

"For everybody who points out the warts—for example, we have a ways to go with metrics—it's easy to forget all the things that have gone so well and helped us get to where we are and really make this such a meaningful way not only to share information but sometimes to save lives," he says.

"From my perspective, for all of us who have been deeply engaged in this, it's a big privilege and a big responsibility to get it right."

Epilogue

I LOVE MY JOB. We should all experience the rush I feel each day when I evangelize on behalf of the mobile industry and, of course, my employer Hipcricket.

But there is one thing that frustrates me. It is the perception that as marketers we don't know enough about mobile to make confident and wise decisions. Nothing could be further from the truth.

From resources mentioned in this book like the Pew Internet & American Life Project to InsightExpress and the Mobile Marketing Association to many, many others, there is ample data available to understand consumer behaviors and interests. It's also wise to use history as a guide.

For instance, it has taken more than two decades for text messaging to become a daily activity for well over 200 million Americans young and old. It took technological standardization, cross-carrier transmission, ubiquity on nearly every device sold, affordable pricing, and a tipping point.

I'll argue that Johnny and Tiffany created the tipping point for text messaging. In your family or circle of friends, they might be named Steve and Jill, but the point is that Johnny and Tiffany are representative of those young people who don't even know that a phone has a voice capability. Yet their mom or aunt or grandpa needs to pick up the kids at soccer practice, and the only way to reach them is via text.

So who do you think becomes the fastest growing segment of texters? Boomers and older generations.

The point is that we should learn from history and not expect the newest, shiniest innovation to be the key to your business success.

Does the newest, shiniest innovation belong in your marketing plan?

Like everything else, it depends.

A case in point? Augmented reality is defined in Wikipedia as "the term for a live direct or indirect view of a physical, real-world environment whose elements are augmented by computer-generated sensory input such as sound, video, graphics, or GPS (global positioning system) data".

Like many things in mobile, augmented reality is meaningful in Asia. On one hand, you have cool technology when you can overlay imaginary things on top of a real scene. But we as a mass group don't even know it exists, even after the holiday season of 2011, when Starbucks introduced Cup Magic.

In case you missed it, customers who downloaded an app for iPhone and Android devices were able to experience augmented reality Starbucks-style. Specifically, by firing up the app and pointing it at a holiday cup, one could interact with five characters—an ice skater, a squirrel, a boy and a dog sledding, and a fox—on their screen.

The object, Alexandra Wheeler, vice president of global digital marketing for Starbucks, told the website *Mashable*, was to "surprise and delight" customers during the holiday season.

Is there a place for "surprise and delight" in mobile? Certainly. Did Starbucks sell more lattes or venti drip coffees as a result of the initiative? It didn't say. In Starbucks's defense, it had previously released mobile products, including an application for its customers to find a location, manage their Starbucks card balance, reload their card, track their standing in the My Starbucks Rewards program, and send a friend an e-gift.

"There's always going to be a shiny object in mobile," says Michael Becker, North America managing director for the Mobile Marketing Association. "I would encourage marketers to take a piece from the Coca-Cola book. I believe it's 70 percent of what is at scale and works now, 20 percent is the next level of reach, and 10 percent is next generation of innovation (i.e., the shiny ball).

"For a marketer, you have to be looking at all three and that's not easy to do. You need to be aligning the majority of budget to that that gets you the broader reach. The second level of your budget to for what will be in the next number of months or next number of quarters, and the third level is paying attention to the shiny ball."

In other words, when it comes to augmented reality and other new shiny mobile things, just because you can doesn't mean that you should.

So what should you do?

A major influencer on Twitter recently posed a question—"What's the coolest thing in mobile?"

My response to him was the Ford program detailed earlier in the book that produced a 14 percent lead conversion rate.

The answer back was that the initiative keyed by a text messaging call to action was an excellent example of a "meat and potatoes" execution.

I'm a vegetarian but will happily dine on "meat and potatoes" mobile programs all day and all night if they produce results that move the needle for my clients.

Mobile works if we're smart about it.

This book has been a career highlight for me. Here's what else is on my mind after researching and writing *Mobilized Marketing*:

Easy Peasy

I humbly offer some unsolicited advice to the mobile industry:

Ladies and gentlemen, every day when you come to your desks, whiteboards, and assembly lines, think of just two words: easy peasy.

For those who need four, how about easy peasy lemon squeezie?

Huh, you say?

How about we rally around the children's rhyme to stop the insanity of metered data plans, crazy distribution points, and even crazier product line introductions?

Has anyone stopped to think that text messaging became a mass activity and super easy (if not easy peasy) when unlimited plans were produced? Now we're asking mobile subscribers to count "MBs" and "GBs."

Yeah, yeah . . . you can go to a website or send a text and get an update, but who has the time or interest to do that?

As for head-scratching distribution points, $99 netbooks with Wi-Fi connections flew off the shelves of retailer CVS. Wonderful, you say? Awful, I say.

How can we possibly provide satisfying customer experiences when we offer low-end, less intuitive products at a drugstore?

Pass the antacid.

And about those wacky product lines? Dell has announced that it would release a "whole slew" of devices—3-, 4-, 7-, 10-inchers. Hopefully, they will all be available in drugstores so consumers won't have to make a separate trip for an aspirin. Just how will a consumer know which model is best? As a colleague said to me, how about we ask them to buy the whole set?

The Need to Say Please

As children, we learn the concept of permission. We know to ask—and say please even—and we understand that others should treat us the same way. So, why is it some marketers don't follow these rules when they engage with consumers? U.S. regulators have floated a Do Not Track proposal for Web users aimed at enabling them to stop advertisers from tracking them online.

The issue came up around mobile during the 2011 holiday season when it was reported that certain retailers were tracking customers.

Marketing is more common sense than brain surgery. The idea of giving consumers what they want—and nothing more—is simple. Permission-based programs are the future (in my view, they are the present as well). Tracking people online or mobile (particularly without transparency into the process) flies in the face of this practice and does anything but encourage interaction between people and brands.

So I ask myself: Why is it so difficult for some marketers to understand the requirement for permission-based marketing—let alone implement permission-based programs?

With Mobile Comes Responsibility

I'm old enough to have gotten my news from Walter Cronkite. Now it comes from @fillintheblank. And @fillintheblank hardly has the gray hair, much less the resume, to warrant the job.

Like many, I learned about the horrific Arizona shooting of Congresswoman Gabrielle Giffords in January 2011 via Twitter. First it was reported that she had died. Then she hadn't.

It immediately took me to the 1980s and my days as a wire service reporter. For some reason, I thought of the time when someone called our newsroom to say that Frank Sinatra had been shot dead by his wife. Only he hadn't.

But if Twitter (and mobile) provided the megaphone those days, might someone have jumped at the faulty information and created a story, not to mention heartbreak in the Sinatra family and beyond?

After the awful shooting of Rep. Giffords, I was left with more questions than answers. Was someone—or more than one— irresponsible or reckless in reporting the news that spread amazingly fast on Twitter and the Web? After all, the tweets primarily came from reports from CNN and National Public Radio (NPR), two reputable news organizations hardly known for their poor journalists.

Did personnel at CNN and/or NPR fail at their *Moments of Trust* with us by reporting the incorrect information faster than they would have before the advent of Twitter and the 24-hour news cycle? Does Twitter pressure journalists to rush to judgment?

Who's a journalist anyway? Anyone can be an iReporter, iWitness, or iKnowItAll and have ample channels to report on something as important as life or death.

Suffice it to say that each of us with a voice that can be heard— and that means everyone with a Twitter account, blog, Facebook page, etc.—has to think before pushing the send button.

You never signed up for that task, you say? Tough. It's our responsibility to be responsible.

iDontThinkSo

On a day when a high-profile columnist declared the death of text messaging with Apple's introduction of iMessage, an interview I did focused on the strength of short message service (SMS) marketing programs.

In the morning, the headline read SMS is still mobile's secret weapon.

For that story, I told the reporter that text messaging provides marketers with reach. It hardly is an end-all for marketers, therefore the need for more engaging tactics such as mobile Web, apps, quick response (QR) codes, and multimedia messaging (MMS).

Then, Apple introduced a messaging product that was free to users but limited to those with the company's products. The columnist wrote that Apple's new instant messaging program would spell the end of SMS.

There are many reasons why the writer posted this piece—as link bait (of course, I fell for it), to drive comments (there were 72 three hours after the piece posted as well as more than 900 tweets), or perhaps because he thinks like a tech reporter, not a typical mobile subscriber who texts daily (as a reminder, more than 70 percent of the more than 300 million mobile users in the United States use SMS).

Even Apple can't reverse a mobile trend like SMS in a day, week, month, or year. Like I said, follow behavior rather than fall for hype.

My Beef with Taco Bell's Crisis Management

Back when my hair was dark, the adage was that you could lose the battle for public opinion in two hours. Today? As discussed in *Mobilized Marketing*, it's closer to two minutes, given social networks and mobile devices that work as megaphones.

I still have a beef with Taco Bell, which in 2010 took five weeks to fully respond to claims in a lawsuit that it was using false advertising when it referred to using "seasoned ground beef" or "seasoned beef" in its products.

Taco Bell finally turned to TV commercials after full-page newspaper ads and Twitter and Facebook efforts reached only about half the population. Imagine that? TV for reach. Television that was in its prime when my hair was, well, you know. Taco Bell initially ran full-page ads in national newspapers. They launched a Twitter campaign, and finally turned to Facebook fans with an offer of a free crunchy beef taco.

Missing from Taco Bell's defense was a mobile strategy. Others in the fast food category, like Arby's, have built robust databases and gained customers by providing offers via mobile. Plus, mobile is ideal for immediacy. Maybe Taco Bell will get there with mobile. But when it comes to crisis management, the company's plans lack meat.

Just How Important Are We as Individuals?

Comcast isn't Nordstrom. But can it be? First off, my bad in 2011 when I didn't pay attention to the timing of the early-bird pricing on the Major League Baseball season package. After seeing the $199 price online, I phoned Comcast, my cable television provider for 10 years; I'd been a bundle customer (including Web and phone) for about the past 2 years.

Comcast's customer service rep listened to my ask—to receive the $20 price break—then told me the deal had expired the previous day.

"But I'm a longtime customer, spend a lot of money with you, and have service on six televisions."

Nothing gave so I hung up. An hour later, I called back and asked for a supervisor. The rep went off the line for about 10 minutes only to come back to chastise me for calling back when I was told no. I again asked for a price break—my fault on the late call but I spend about $250 a month with Comcast—and was told it wasn't going to happen.

"How about a $20 credit for being such a good customer?" No and no. I took my story to Twitter and @comcastcares, who quickly responded by asking me to send my story to an e-mail address.

On my answering machine that night, Comcast called to ask me to take a survey about my customer service experience. They don't read their files or Twitter?

The next morning, Executive Customer Care e-mailed me and said in part, "We do value you greatly as a customer and completely understand that in today's economy that there are many ways to obtain entertainment service and it is a choice of our customers to choose Comcast for their phone, Internet, and TV service. We cannot thank you enough for your dedication to us as a company and for helping us keep our commitment to quality customer care. I would like to offer you the MLB season pass, free of charge to you should you still wish to order this package."

Nordstrom-esque, wouldn't you say? Of course, I screwed up initially by failing to call during the introductory pricing period. But I expected to be treated like a valued customer at the brand's *Moments of Trust.*

Not that I was thinking this way, but what if I believed, 'Gosh, I have a lot of Twitter followers, a mobile phone with instant access to social networks, and I want to be treated like royalty'?

Fast forward a few days.

I ended up with a rather uncooked expensive piece of halibut at a nice restaurant near my home. This despite my request to have the halibut cooked medium well rather than the usual medium rare restaurants in the Northwest typically choose to prepare fish. The establishment did not ask me if I was a big shot. It did not (as far as I know) go onto Twitter to see if I have a following. What did it do?

- Apologized profusely.
- Prepared a new piece of fish the way I wanted it cooked.
- Sent me a salad while I was waiting so my wife and I wouldn't eat at separate times.
- Offered us free dessert.
- Took the price of the halibut off the bill (despite the fact that it was the most expensive item).

My point in telling this story? The restaurant performed admirably. It had nothing to do with my clout or any supposed influence that I have. It was purely good business.

Mobile and social networks have changed everything. And nothing.

How Big?

The group of those who are bullish on mobile and its place in the marketing mix grows every week. And these executives aren't betting on a gut feeling. They have been convinced by real results. Initiatives have moved product, raised brand awareness and engagement, and given marketers more confidence in mobile marketing and mobile advertising. As a result, more money is moving into the mobile channel.

There is at least one agency mobile practice lead who has made the mother of all mobile predictions, saying that the mobile ad spend will overtake television.

To put that into perspective, you need to know that a cool $131 billion was spent on television advertising in the United States alone in 2010. By comparison, JP Morgan predicts that mobile ad spend would reach about $1 billion in the United States in 2011.

The reasons for the executive's optimism? Mobile is the first truly mass media. It beats TV on reach. Mobile is the most adopted technology and media channel in history, with high engagement rates and 24-hour access to users.

And even if some remain disbelievers, the number of brands convinced of the power of mobile is on the rise. Driven by increased client budgets, the mobile practice of the executive's agency has grown dramatically.

In the 12 years that I spent working in advertising and public relations firms, I did not see agencies increase head count if they didn't have the client work to back it up. The agency model is to win business, then staff against it. I'm not privy to the mobile agency's revenue, but I do know the firm is very active and certainly wouldn't staff up wildly in the hopes of winning business. As for the executive's prediction, he certainly has good reason to believe mobile will be huge. I also know that mobile is going to be big, but forecasting too far out is problematic for me.

We'll continue to watch the growth of mobile and comment. You are invited and encouraged to be part of the conversation. Please join me on Twitter @jeffhasen and at www.jeffhasen.com.

About the Author

Named a top chief marketing officer (CMO) on Twitter, Jeff Hasen (@jeffhasen) builds, strengthens, and protects brands. Companies benefiting from his talents have landed on *Wired*'s list of most innovative entities on Earth and been named pioneers and the early leader in the burgeoning mobile marketing category.

One of the most frequently quoted voices in mobile and social media, Jeff cocreated the certification program for the Mobile Marketing Association (MMA). He frequently trains marketers and others on mobile's definitions, techniques, and benefits. Jeff is a member of the MMA's Consumer Best Practices Committee.

As CMO, he has seen Hipcricket to a public market listing; designation by CTIA–The Wireless Association as a pioneer and by a leading wireless analyst as an "industry powerhouse"; and sale. Attesting to the strength of his efforts, the acquiring company now sells its products and services under the Hipcricket brand to such companies as MillerCoors, Macy's, Nestlé, and Clear Channel, among many Fortune 500 companies as well as hundreds of others.

For InfoSpace, he drove a repositioning of the 10-year-old company from 1 percent share player in online search to the pioneer in mobile media and to No. 20 on the prestigious Wired 40 list of most innovative companies on Earth.

Through his *Moments of Trust* lessons, he teaches marketers to interact with consumers who are armed with a mobile device and a voice that can instantly change or reinforce public opinion.

Jeff spent the first 12 years of his career as a journalist for United Press International. He holds a bachelor of arts degree in television and radio from Brooklyn College.

He is a frequent speaker at industry events and writes for *Mobile Marketer*, imediaconnection.com, Technorati.com, ideamensch.com, and mobilegroove.com, among others. More at jeffhasen.com and on Twitter @jeffhasen.

Index